For our grandchildren
Sebastien, Katarina and Antoinette
May their world be blessed with
Greater kindness and wisdom

*Without engagement,
liberal democracy can't survive.*

*Healthy democracy is about
living with disagreement,
not eliminating it.*

*Restoring the ability to disagree without becoming
mortal enemies is a new and urgent civic imperative.*

Michael R. Bloomberg
former Mayor, City of New York

Preface

"Capitalism for Democrats" came out in October 2019. In its first few months, it showed that it needed a companion volume—"Capitalism for America". Why? It became clear that the message was universal. We found it being embraced by people far to the right of what we expected, who said, yes, that's how we think. The left had more trouble with it. But even there, it received affectionate praise and the hope that it could help to bring Americans together.

Capitalism for America therefore is my attempt to describe a capitalism that the vast majority of Americans can agree is the economic system we want. Such a consensus would not, of course, end disagreements about economics, but it would focus our disagreements on the productive work of deciding what will work best for the American people within a framework of market capitalism and a determination to strive for fairness within that system.

It is true that the Great Recession and Great Financial Crisis of 2007-09 revealed defects in capitalism that have persuaded many Americans—and particularly young Democrats—to reject capitalism as the proper foundation for America's economic system. Those reactions are understandable, even though excessive debt can bring grief under any economic system.

Maybe it would be right to reject capitalism if the only choices were between crony capitalism, "free market" "laissez-faire" capitalism, and some other, apparently fairer, economic system, maybe called socialism.

Fortunately, those are not the only choices. There is a capitalism that works to the benefit of substantially all people. This book was written to describe that capitalism in a way that should be accessible to readers and acceptable to the vast majority of Americans.

Unfortunately, in our bifurcated political arena, many Americans have not been exposed to the sound practical, moral and philosophical bases for that kind of capitalism.

That is not their fault. The press and academic pundits tend to occupy the more extreme positions on the left and right. For young progressives, the writings of the right that exalt free markets are easy to dismiss because they so clearly lead to exploitation by the moneyed

i

classes. The writers on the left seem to make more sense to them—at least the writers on the left have some empathy. And in the academy, the left is largely ascendant.

Missing are the pundits and commentators in the middle. It is harder to keep writing columns that people want to read if you are not sensational, or at least angry. Sensation and anger sell newspapers, as they say—and they draw people to their TV screens and their social media as well. We centrists often sound sappy anyway, I suppose.

This little book asks Americans of all political persuasions to take a few hours out of their busy lives to consider what capitalism has accomplished, what it can accomplish, why it has a moral basis, and why it is in the best interests of the nation for it to continue to be our governing economic theory—so long as it is properly aided by laws and regulations that protect consumers and workers and the competitive markets through which they speak.

Basically, capitalism works because it empowers billions of individual decisions that we call "the market" to allocate resources (through the price mechanism of consumer choice) rather than giving power to elites to make those decisions for the rest of us. To accomplish that virtuous allocation, capitalism must be supported by regulation that preserves competition and assures that consumers can make informed choices. Capitalism does not regulate itself.

If you are looking for simple answers, you won't find them here. The world is complex. But in a democracy, people should try to understand these complexities.

In studying the intellectual background of capitalism, I am indebted to Jerry Z. Muller, a professor at Catholic University in Washington, D.C., whose magisterial *The Mind and The Market* is a trove first of historical information and then of commonsensical analysis. I cite Professor Muller's book many times because, as he said, "The question of the market—of its moral significance, of its social, political, cultural, and economic ramifications—has been at the focus of modern European [and, he might have added, American] thought." (p. 388)

I come to writing this book as a veteran lawyer, banker, entrepreneur, and writer on economic subjects. I have investigated and written about the major financial debacles of the last half-century, so I have no illusions. I have written two books and numerous articles on corporate governance over the last 50 years, so whether or not I have the right ideas on that subject, at least I have given it a lot of thought.

My books that I will refer to in this book are *Debt Spiral*, (about the causes of the Great Recession and Great Financial Crisis), *Instability* (that describes how financial systems are naturally unstable), *High Rollers* (a history of the savings and loan debacle), and *The Education Solution* (why we need better early education in order to enable less affluent children to enter kindergarten equally prepared as more affluent children). *The Education Solution* also has a website: www.the-education-solution.com.

Part of my preparation for this book—and for my other writings—is reading several newspapers each day (though not every word, of course)—some online and some in hard copy. These include The New York Times, Wall Street Journal, Financial Times, Bloomberg.com, and my local newspaper The Tampa Bay Times. I would also read the Washington Post, the Los Angeles Times and the Boston Globe, but time is limited. I also look at a number of websites frequently, including think tanks left, right and center and the official Chinese news service.

I am a lifelong centrist Democrat. I am an old white guy. But I still have some useful things to say.

I greatly respect the young people who question the utility and morality of capitalism. Neither capitalism nor any other system of economic governance is perfect. But despite capitalism's defects, the argument in favor of market capitalism is persuasive. I hope you will agree.

A Few Words about Footnotes and Sources

In order to enhance readability, this book has no footnotes or citations, except to books and restricted access articles. The citations to these are contained in the text. The citations to other materials—all of which can be accessed online—are available at our website CapitalismForAmerica.net. The citations there identify my sources in a clickable format. You should be able readily to check my sources using that mechanism. The website also has other resources you may want to use.

In 1975
Time Magazine wondered
whether capitalism could survive
the deep recession of 1974 75.
It could and it did.

Table of Contents

Introduction

Competitive Markets Make Capitalism Work

This book explains that capitalism is moral, that it works, and that its defects can be remediated within its basic framework. It is not my purpose to bash socialism or any other economic theory.

Basically, capitalism works because it empowers billions of individual decisions that we call "the market" to allocate resources (through the price mechanism of consumer choice) rather than giving power to elites to make those decisions for the rest of us. To accomplish that virtuous allocation, capitalism must be supported by regulation that preserves competition and, most importantly, that enables consumers to make informed choices. Capitalism does not regulate itself.

That basic theory is simple. Regulating capitalism so that it works for real human beings is the complex part.

Markets are pragmatically better than elites at allocating resources. They are morally superior to elites for exercising that power, as well. The moral basis is just as important as the pragmatic one.

Today, not only is capitalism under attack from those who prefer some type of "socialism", but among advocates of capitalism there also is a struggle between those who proclaim that capitalism must be based on "free markets" and those who believe that capitalism should be based on carefully regulated "competitive markets". I will argue that competitive markets produce the capitalism we want, whereas the free market mantra leads to a perversion that favors the moneyed classes.

In the course of this discussion, I find myself, out of necessity, on Humpty Dumpty's side of his argument with Alice (in Wonderland):

"When I use a word," Humpty Dumpty said, in rather a scornful tone, "it means just what I choose it to mean—neither more nor less."

"The question is," said Alice, "whether you can make words mean so many different things."

"The question is," said Humpty, "which is to be master."

Several key words in this essay, such as capitalism, socialism, and humanism, have been used to mean so many different things that in order to use them, one has to select one of many available definitions. As the writer of this essay, I must be master of those definitions, regardless of whether the reader's favorite usage is different.

A Global Inflection Point in Governance

The definitions are important. But the global context in which our choice of economic system now takes place is equally important—and that context may not yet be sufficiently clear.

Capitalism has been a part of what has been called the "post-World War II liberal consensus" that has brought peace to the nations of Europe and the rest of the world, except for civil wars and big-power interventions in those civil wars. (Those civil wars and big-power interventions have been bad enough, I grant, but not as bad as great power conflicts.) That liberal consensus—and the capitalism that is a part of it—also has brought the greatest improvement in people's economic well being in all of history.

These things have been accomplished by cooperation among nations that also is unprecedented. Cooperation has included world trade organizations, regional trade and governance organizations, UN agencies, mutual defense pacts, and numerous other forms of cooperation. Cooperation, like all human institutions, never is perfect, but imperfect cooperation beats no cooperation over any extended period of time.

The liberal consensus no longer can be said to be ascendant, however. Narrow nationalism, autocracy and an oxymoron called illiberal democracy are ascendant in many nations, and with that ascendancy, the multi-nation understandings are in danger as well because autocrats tend to reject multi-nation agreements in favor of beggar-thy-neighbor policies based on individual power rather than mutual benefit.

President Trump has taken America in that beggar-thy-neighbor direction, but many other governments have gone as far or farther.

Russia is number one. But European nations such as Poland, Hungary and Italy, as well as Turkey and Brazil, to name a few that have abandoned the multilateral consensus, also denigrate the benefits of cooperation. (China, as so often, is a special case. At least rhetorically, it embraces multilateral organizations, but it has an autocratic form of government and its sincerity can be challenged.) Even in the U.K., the birthplace of philosophical liberalism, the leaders of three leading parties all have rejected the liberal consensus.

President Putin of Russia is the "leader of the pack". In July 2019, he pronounced liberalism dead. It is "obsolete", he averred. Nationalism and the pursuit of individual national interests are now ascendant—and properly so, he said.

In the kind of world that President Putin embraces—and that numerous other national leaders embrace—the chances of war among great powers are rising, the trade that has enhanced people's well being all over the world is shrinking, and economic progress and cooperation will wither.

As I will explain, capitalism—the good capitalism—is a liberal form of economic governance that is an important aspect of liberal governance in general. Whether America continues to be a capitalist nation is likely to be an important part of whether President Putin turns out to be on the right side of history or on the wrong side. The outcome of the contest between multi-national liberalism and beggar-thy-neighbor nationalism will depend on which one people want and will vote for.

Liberal governance has been challenged before, most notably in the two world wars. The current situation is not yet a shooting war—and I hope it never will be that—but to prevent it from becoming that, we probably need to begin by restoring the United States of America to being a liberal land that values other people, not just Americans, as well as improving on America's many defects.

In that regard, I must ask the question: "Do Americans have enough confidence in their own system to stick to or return to policies that have brought us great prosperity and the respect of the world?" Responding to my question by email recently, Martin Wolf, Chief Economics Correspondent for the FT, was dubious: "Americans have lost belief in your own virtues", he said. "It is a great tragedy."

"The liberal capitalist model has delivered peace, prosperity and technological progress for the past 50 years, dramatically reducing poverty and raising living standards throughout the world.

At times, it is necessary to reform in order to preserve. Today, the world has reached that moment."

- Lionel Barber, Editor, Financial Times
September 16, 2019

CHAPTER 1

The Attacks on Capitalism

That capitalism is under attack in America is not news.

Peggy Noonan (Ronald Reagan's speechwriter and a regular Saturday columnist in the Wall Street Journal) has opined that, "an entire generation has risen since the crash of 2008. They've never even heard a defense of capitalism. They've never heard anyone speak well of it."

David Brooks (a more centrist Republican who publishes in The New York Times) says: "As the recovery has advanced, people's faith in capitalism has actually declined, especially among the young. Only 45 percent of those between 18 and 29 see capitalism positively, a lower rate than in 2010, when the country was climbing out of the Great Recession."

Noah Smith, a left-leaning columnist at Bloomberg.com, has written that:

"When even leading economists are questioning the very idea of capitalism, you know the system is in trouble. In a recent article, Nobel economics winner Angus Deaton reviewed two books by other distinguished economists -- Raghuram Rajan and Paul Collier -- that argue that capitalism is fundamentally flawed. Rajan laments the demise of local communities in the face of big government and mass markets, while Collier discusses the tendency of meritocracy to concentrate talent and money. Meanwhile, income and wealth inequality is at the center of the well-known critique of capitalism by economist Thomas Piketty. Some critics of capitalism argue that the problem is monopoly power, while others say that capitalism is the culprit behind climate change.

Steven Pearlstein, whose book *Can American Capitalism Survive?* is cited by many progressives, says at the outset:

"In less than a generation, what was once considered the optimal system for organizing economic activity is now widely viewed, at home and abroad, as having betrayed its ideals and purpose and forfeited its moral legitimacy." (p. 3)

I will discuss Pearlstein's book in several chapters because he is an intelligent and knowledgeable critic of capitalism.

"I'm a capitalist and even I think capitalism is broken," said billionaire hedge fund manager Ray Dalio.

Prominent commentators from the center-left also have noted the scarcity of recent defenses of capitalism. John Authers, then with the Financial Times but now with Bloomberg.com, who I regard as an excellent observer, opined on May 11, 2018 that: "People in America—and in other parts of the developed world where the same effects are at work but less pronounced—are fed up with CEOs chasing the bottom line and they are fed up with capitalism."

Not every CEO of an S&P 500 company is lavishly compensated. Some voluntarily dial back their pay. But a majority are very highly compensated.

President Trump proclaimed in his State of the Union address on February 6, 2019, "Tonight, we renew our resolve that America will never be a Socialist country." But back in July 2018, The Mises Institute decried Trump's bailout of farmers as "Trump's road to socialism".

Are the President, the Mises Institute, and the young Democrats thinking about the same thing when they use the word "socialism"? In any particular case, it is hard to know. Later on, I will explore the general question of what the word socialism may mean to different people.

The future of capitalism has been questioned at many times in recent American history. For example, in 1975 *Time Magazine* had a featured article, "Can Capitalism Survive?" It can, and it did.

And in 1990, many in the West saw the Japanese combination of capitalism and a strong state industrial policy as the best future form of economic organization. As unearthed by Bloomberg's John Authers, William S. Dietrich said in his 1990 book *The Shadow of the Rising Sun*:

>"Boasts about the victory of free-market capitalism in the wake of the collapse of the Communist state-directed system are premature and distract attention from the necessary recognition that it is the Japanese combination of the free market with a strong central state and a highly skilled professional bureaucracy that has really proved triumphant in our modern age of advanced technology. Only if we fully understand the reasons for Japanese success and American decline can we begin the arduous but crucial task of reconstructing the American polity to give it the power required to formulate and implement a national industrial

policy that can regain for the United States its preeminent place among the world's industrial powers.

"The alternative, Dietrich describes in a chilling scenario, is a "Pax Nipponica" that will find America playing second fiddle to Japan with economic, cultural, and political consequences that will make Britain's eclipse by the United States earlier in this century seem mild by comparison."

Yet by ten years later, Japan had suffered its "lost decade" and the U.S. had experienced a decade of great prosperity without any increase in state control of the economy. As often has been the case, forecasts of the demise of capitalism have been off the mark. State control actually did Japan no good in the long run because it sapped the entrepreneurial spirit.

Nevertheless, numerous economists and politicians, both on the right and on the left, today are advocating an American "industrial policy" that sounds like the policies of Japan in the 1970s and 1980s in order for America's manufacturing to compete with China (usually by means of government subsidies). Those proposals suggest to me a lack of confidence in capitalism, even among many Republicans. (More on industrial policy in Chapter 11.)

Bases of the Recent Attacks

The recent attacks on capitalism in the west—and particularly in America—arise principally in three categories:

1. Rapacious bankers take advantage of the rest of us and cause busts like the Great Financial Crisis.

2. The top management class exploits the workers by siphoning off an unwarranted share of the profits.

3. Capitalism does not provide sufficient protections for workers and for people who get left behind.

I will discuss these attacks in greater detail later, but here is briefly why I agree that these attacks ring true:

1. *Rapacious bankers.*

Not all bankers are rapacious. But rapacious bankers are an important symptom of what can happen if capitalism (or any other form of economic governance) is allowed to run amok, which the "free market" mantra tends to permit. Rapacious bankers are a perversion of capitalism—and an important perversion to prevent.

2 *Self-aggrandizing top managements.*

I agree with the conventional wisdom: many American CEOs are paid too much. Data from the Financial Times newspaper (FT), for example, show that CEOs are paid something on the order of 300 times as much as ordinary workers—and that that is not a recent phenomenon. The big jump from about 50 times to about 300 times worker pay came in the 1990s.

The U.S. is alone in paying CEOs so much. In Germany, for example, CEOs are paid about half as much, and other advanced country companies tend to pay less than German companies. It is that appearance of unfairness that drives people's understandable anger. Other than out of vanity—really—who needs to make that much money?

My own statistical work, however, suggests that American top executives are not paid money that otherwise would provide workers with a significantly better lifestyle. I did a study of the 20 U.S. companies with the largest numbers of employees. It showed that if the top five officers of those companies were paid *nothing* and their pay were distributed pro rata among their employees, each employee would net about $100 per year. Thus, while the complaint about CEO compensation is understandable (I agree they are paid too much), its symbolism is more important than its economic impact on workers.

The problem that stands in the way of higher employee compensation is (as my study showed) that the biggest employers are not among the most profitable companies. They may not be able to afford significantly higher pay, given the businesses they are in and the ways they have chosen to compete. Maybe they should radically change the way businesses, but usually that is extremely difficult and dangerous.

Supermarket giant Kroger, for example, embarked on an ambitious program to modernize its business. But as the Wall Street Journal reported on November 21, 2019, "Kroger Co. is turning back to the basics of selling groceries after trying to sell too many new products and renovate too many stores at once."

"The supermarket operator is navigating a tough conundrum: how to bring its stores and e-commerce operations up to speed while pressure to compete on price is tougher than ever. Kroger is facing increased competition from all sides. Discounters including Aldi and Lidl are expanding, putting pressure on Kroger to keep prices low. At the higher end of the market, regional grocers like Publix Super Markets Inc. and

Wegmans Food Markets Inc. are increasing their sales more rapidly than Kroger."

The most profitable companies *do* pay better than supermarkets do, but they also are in quite different types of business and have more highly educated workforces. Competition for grocery sales is ferocious.

A complaint that frequently parallels the self-aggrandizing CEOs complaint is a complaint that corporate boards are too shortsighted and therefore invest too little in the long-term future of their companies. That allegation tends to lead to demands for redefinition of the legal obligations of corporate directors. I will discuss that issue in Chapter 6 on "Corporate Governance".

3. Insufficient worker protections and safety net.

Capitalism does not, in theory, say anything about how to help those who get left behind in the competitive marketplace. That kind of assistance is a governmental overlay. And in America, the government does not, in my opinion, provide sufficient protections for workers or a sufficient safety net. A carefully crafted and adequate safety net would be consistent with capitalism.

Some commentators (and some candidates) complain, however, that the more basic problem is that Americans make less money than workers in other advanced nations. The problem, they aver, is "pre-distribution" rather than a need for better "redistribution". Probably there is some truth in that assertion. It appears, however, that on a comparative basis, the lack of a sufficient American safety net is the bigger cause of the differential in aggregate results between the U.S. and other advanced countries.

In April 2019, Martin Wolf of the FT published data that strongly suggested that the difference between the GINI coefficients of the U.S. and other advanced nations is due to less safety net redistribution, not less market income. (The GINI coefficient is a measure frequently used to compare relative levels of inequality.) On market income, American inequality was about on a par with other nations' (except for Sweden, Canada and Switzerland, which are more egalitarian in their market income), but that after considering taxes and transfers, the U.S. is more unequal than the other nations. The reasons that the inequality grows are that the U.S. has a smaller safety net and fewer benefits provided by the government.

Data like these suggest to me that the most realistic ways to attack the American inequality problem are by increasing the level and types of government assistance and by instituting long-term educational policies to increase the ability of more Americans to qualify for high-paying jobs.

Almost daily, one sees articles claiming that a college education really is not worth its cost. Those articles do not take honest account of the data. College-educated people do better in life generally, as well as economically. And post-high-school education aimed at particular careers also usually is of value.

The anti-education articles are written by people on the right who know that college educated people are more likely to vote Democratic and by people on the left who yearn for the days when people with less education could earn a good living. Those days are not coming back, simply because the nature of work has changed so much.

Donald Sassoon, in *The Anxious Triumph: A Global History of Capitalism 1860-2014* (Allen Lane 2019) offers (at p.512) an explanation of why wealthy capitalists are so reviled:

"[R]ich capitalists are more disliked than the aristocracy of old, since being born an aristocrat like being born rich is a matter of luck like winning the lottery, while self made capitalists suggest that those who did not make it were incompetent or lazy."

Sounds plausible to me.

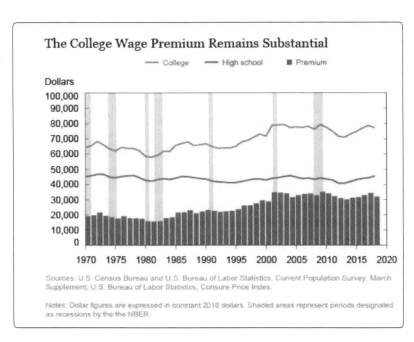

CHAPTER 2

Trust in People's Decision-Making Defines Capitalism

The capitalist system trusts that ordinary people in the aggregate, acting as they see their own best interests, will make better economic decisions than experts or elites can make. As such, it is a liberal humanist philosophy that relies on and exalts ordinary citizens. In the aggregate, they (ordinary citizens) are the market, and their decisions are reflected in prices and resource allocations. As Martin Wolf of the FinancialTimes described it,

"Liberalism is not a precise philosophy, it is an attitude. All liberals . . . trust in the capacity of human beings to decide things for themselves."

David Brooks of the New York Times described liberalism in similar terms:

"Philosophic liberalism . . . begins with intellectual humility. There's more we don't know than we do know, so public life is a constant conversation that has no end. In the liberal view, each person contains opposites and contradictions. You flatten and dehumanize complex individuals when you see people according to crude dichotomies and assign them to tribal teams."

* * *

"Liberalism loves sympathy, suspects rage and detests cruelty.
Politics is inevitably a dialogue between partial truths."

The Irish poet W.B. Yeats wrote a seminal poem called "The Second Coming" in 1919 against the backdrop of the historical inflection point of the First World War, the Russian Revolution and the Irish Easter Rising. Here is its central theme:

Things fall apart; the centre cannot hold;
Mere anarchy is loosed upon the world
The blood-dimmed tide is loosed, and everywhere

11

The ceremony of innocence is drowned;
The best lack all conviction, while the worst
Are full of passionate intensity.

The Corn Flakes Example

How does the market process work? How do ordinary consumer decisions about which corn flakes to buy get reflected in prices and resource allocations?

The process is not mysterious. As consumers, we just don't think about—or sometimes even realize—our collective power.

Say you go to the grocery store and corn flakes is on your list. It is what you like to eat for breakfast.

To simplify, there are two kinds of corn flakes on the shelf: a name brand such as Kellogg's® and a store brand, we'll call it Generic Corn Flakes. A 16-ounce package of Generic Corn Flakes costs a dollar less than the Kellogg's version, so although you have eaten Kellogg's all your life (they have been available since 1894!), you decide to save the money by trying a box of Generic.

You eat the Generic Corn Flakes and find they are just as good as Kellogg's. So you tell your friends—mostly online of course. And gradually, Kellogg's sells less and less corn flakes, as people discover that the brand is just hype.

Now Kellogg's has decisions to make. Should it reduce prices? Can it reduce prices and remain profitable, given its cost structure? Should it change its marketing approach? Kellogg's has to do something—and whatever that some thing is, it will have an impact on the Kellogg Company and on its supply chain. And whatever those impacts are, they will have been caused by what you and your friends and their friends etc. have done. That is capitalism in action.

The same sort of thing would have happened if you had decided that Generic Corn Flakes were not nearly as good as Kellogg's. You would tell about your experience, and, gradually, Generic Corn Flakes would sell less and less. Then the manufacturers of Generic and the stores that sell them would have decisions to make. Do they try to improve taste? Do they cut prices even further? Or do they abandon the cornflakes business altogether? And those decisions will reverberate down the Generic manufacturer's supply chain. And again, all this will take place because of what you and your friends did. And it will be capitalism in action.

The same thing does not happen in a system where decisions are made by elites. Elites are likely to say that choice is wasteful—and only Generic Corn Flakes are needed. So no Kellogg's are on the shelves.

But Kellogg's still are on the shelves in some other country. And Kellogg's Corn Flakes lovers will find a way get them "on the black market". They will cost more, but there likely will be a black market in many things.

I hope that cornflakes example helps consumers to understand how much power they really have in a capitalist economy.

Consumers Need Regulation to Assure They Can Be Informed

The humanist philosophy behind capitalism relies, however, on sound regulation of the naturally selfish interests of market participants. For example, to allocate resources efficiently, people—the decision-makers in the market—have to make *informed* decisions. Thus, for example, the banks that misled borrowers and investors *perverted* the capitalist system; they took advantage of human frailties for their own benefit. (I will postpone my Humpty Dumpty moment defining "humanism" until later.)

There are many stories about how people who were buying homes or refinancing them were tricked into taking loans they could not afford. The big banks often were at the end of the money supply line, but between the big banks and the borrowers there were numerous intermediaries, and often it was those closest to the borrowers—the local mortgage brokers— who did the worst of the dirty work.

The big banks also committed fraud, but their fraud was mostly on the institutions—many of them European rather than American— who bought the securities that they packaged using the mortgage obligations that the local mortgage brokers had sold. Everyone, it seemed, had a reason to pretend and mislead in order to make money.

The Consumer Finance Protection Bureau (CFPB)—that Senator Elizabeth Warren and I and many others campaigned for—was established after the Great Recession to prevent banks and others similarly situated from continuing to mislead customers.

The CFPB's job—which is making sure that customers are informed and not misled—is vital to protecting capitalism from powerful parties who think it in their self-interest to mislead consumers.

In addition, discrimination of any sort (such as race, sex or sexual orientation) that is based on non-market data also is anathema to market capitalism, since it distorts the aggregate of market decision-making.

As these observations indicate, market capitalism requires that providers of goods and services compete to flourish through the informed affirmative votes of consumers. As researchers at the centrist think tank Brookings Institution observed in 2018,

> "Thus, competition allows the market economy to allocate resources efficiently. Without it, there can be distortions that reduce overall welfare, as concentrated interests benefit at the expense of the broader public."

Consumer knowledge—and therefore producer disclosure and fair dealing—is at the heart of capitalist theory. Without accurate consumer information, the theory of capitalism is bankrupt. This book will not attempt to detail how the laws should achieve that goal. But the principle of consumer protection is the great dividing line between pro-competitive- market people like me (and, I hope, you will agree, too) and "free market" adherents like former Federal Reserve Board Chairman Greenspan and some of my friends at conservative think tanks.

Does Capitalism Depend on Consumers Being Rational?

The rational expectations hypothesis that formed the basis for much 20th century capitalist economic theory has come under attack in recent years. Regardless of whether that attack is sound, I ask: "Does capitalism have to assume that people are rational?" And I answer that that depends on what we mean by "rational".

Rational cannot mean that people are not tempted by cashew nuts. That is a natural human response, and therefore it is presumptively rational, even if it is unhealthy. See the work of Nobelist Richard Thaler of the University of Chicago for more on the cashew temptation.

Capitalism also does not have to assume that any single individual is rational—only that people are, in the aggregate, rational. And capitalism does not have to assume that any person has complete knowledge or even that people in the aggregate, on average, have complete knowledge. As British economist Roger Farmer has put it, "Individuals are not irrational, they are simply acting on incomplete knowledge, a situation that is shared by policy makers in national treasuries and central banks."

The future is not knowable, and even the sum of the past cannot be known by any single person. Thus, rational actions may take a range of forms, all of which are legitimate in the eyes of capitalist theory. And as Roger Farmer said, although a central banker, such as a member of the Fed, may have more information than most people, they nevertheless have incomplete information and cannot foresee the future.

In an economic sense, whether something is "rational" is not objectively verifiable. Rationality is, instead, a concept that we ascribe to human decision-making in general, not to particular outcomes. Although any single person may be irrational, the sum of people's decision-making cannot, we may say, by definition, be *not* rational. It may be wrong in hindsight, but if it is the product of an informed market, it cannot have been irrational.

I just had a Humpty Dumpty moment, you say? I re-defined "rational". I guess so. I think the rational expectations hypothesis discussion has suffered from arguments about its meaning in the air. Maybe I have defined it into oblivion. But maybe it belongs there.

Capitalism, Humanism, and the Industrial Revolution

A defense of capitalism should include the historical perspective, which tends to substantiate capitalism's liberal, humanist roots.

Capitalism, the Enlightenment and the Industrial Revolution all commenced at about the time that the U.S. was founded. When Adam Smith's *Wealth of Nations* was published and the American Revolution began in 1776, the Industrial Revolution already was under way to an extent, but its pace accelerated in the 19th century, perhaps owing to the birth of capitalism.

Before the 19th century, commerce was closely managed by governments, and almost all governments were monarchies. Companies, few of which had limited liability structures, had to be authorized by the Crown (or Parliament) and were allowed to conduct business only at the discretion of the Crown. The more liberal availability of the limited liability company structure that grew during the 19th century, particularly in the U.S. and England, enabled businesses to obtain private financing for projects that the financial markets decided were worthwhile. At the same time, removal of strict price controls that had been imposed by the Crown (or Parliament) and liberalization of the right to sell goods into a variety of (formerly closed) markets enabled merchants to sell their goods relatively free of governmental restraints.

Markets, both for capital and for goods and services, are a key component of what we have come to call capitalism. The democratic nations of the U.S., England and (sometimes) France were in the vanguard of this liberalization, and their economies flourished as a result. Nations that remained fettered by monarchical governments tended not to trust the market idea enough to take full advantage of its benefits.

Adam Smith, who sometimes is called the father of capitalism, was first and foremost what I would call a humanist, though neither my meaning of "humanist" nor the terms "capitalism" or "economist" seem to have been in common use as early as 1776. ("Capitalism" seems to have appeared in the mid-19th century. "Economist" in the modern sense is a 20th century coining, though the term "political economy" goes back to the 19th century.) Capitalism, even without that name, suited Smith's humanist instincts. The great economic thinkers of the next century were humanists as well, with John Stuart Mill being the figure who most stood out as both an economic thinker and a humanist.

The terms humanist and humanism are important to this essay, so I will have another Humpty Dumpty moment and state my definition, while recognizing that many definitions have been used over the two centuries that the term has been in general use.

By humanist, I mean the most general definition of the term: a person who bases philosophy on "the general love of humanity". Wikipedia attributes the first use of "humanist" to a French writer in 1765. Britannica attributes it to German scholars in the 19th century.

Beginning in the 18th century "intellectuals set themselves the task of developing a political and social theory that would allow those of radically different visions of the good and holy life to live together. Such a theory would also protect intellectual humanists steeped in multiple religions and national cultures from the depredations of religious fanatics." The Mind and the Market, p.16.

One of the first prominent uses of the term "humanism" was to describe classical scholars of the Italian Renaissance. Other prominent early uses included anti-religious definitions of humanism—that is, distinguishing between secular humanism and various forms of religion, principally Christian. Yet, curiously, there also have been religious— particularly Protestant—groups that have used "humanist" to describe their own philosophies. I do not adopt the anti-religious sense of the term. Humanism and most religions coexist quite easily.

Given this linguistic potential confusion, it might be better to use some term other than humanism to describe the roots of capitalism. But I have not found another word that adequately would convey the fundamental beliefs that led to capitalism. Therefore please accept my definition of humanism for purposes of this discussion. Britannica, at least, finds it the most legitimate definition.

I also should say something about what I mean by "liberalism". It is not the same thing that today is called progressivism. It is a more old-fashioned concept that speaks to the values that my quotations from David Brooks embody. It is skeptical, caring and universal. They are the values that the Founders embraced when we revolted against autocratic rule. Not every man for himself, but e pluribus unum.

How Capitalism and Its Regulation Derive from Humanism

Humanism is related to capitalism in that capitalism relies on the aggregate actions of people, through markets, to make economic decisions. People are, in fact, the mythical "invisible hand". It should be obvious, then, that asymmetry of information prevents markets from allocating resources the way they are supposed to in order to achieve efficiency. *Thus the most fundamental roles of regulation are to prevent monopolies and to assure that consumers are provided with sufficient accurate information to make decisions in their own best interests.*

Note that in the preceding paragraph I used the word "efficiency" in a specialized way. Although other systems measure efficiency by purportedly objective criteria, market capitalism can make no such claim because its goal is not to satisfy objective criteria but to satisfy the needs of the people as expressed by them through the market mechanism. Thus it is the purity of the process—not someone's objectified evaluation of the results—that determine capitalism's theoretical success or failure. More autocratic societies, by contrast, do not accept the economic will of the people. Instead, authorities decide what is efficient and impose those decisions on the people.

I will repeat one point from the preceding paragraph: capitalism depends on processes, not results. Capitalism enables people to make informed choices. The results are up to the choices that people make, and capitalism does not second-guess the people's determinations.

Market capitalism that relies on people's decisions stands in contrast to systems where economic decisions are made by the fiat of elites. In modern market capitalism, the officers of Apple, for example, have some market power, but it is only market power that has been given to them by the decisions of consumers, assisted by Trademark and Patent laws, and they retain that power only at the sufferance of consumers. They have strong competitors and would lose their power if they did not keep up with consumers' preferences. The iPhone® will be a leading product only as long as consumers make it so. Some day—maybe soon—consumers will consign the iPhone to the dust heap of history, as they eventually have consigned almost every previous product.

By contrast, crony capitalism is not capitalism at all, since it is the state rather than markets that allocates opportunities to cronies. Whether overt or subtle, state actions that allocate markets to the powerful are crony capitalism. Thus the fight for and against crony capitalism never ends. I will discuss it more in Chapter 9. But we should make no mistake: Government takeover by rich cronies is not a problem only of capitalist societies. It is a problem of all societies, regardless of their form of economic organization. Indeed, often the problem is worst in societies such as the Soviet Union, where no one was supposed to be rich, but in fact the well-connected were very rich, while ordinary people had very little.

Humanism, Capitalism and Democracy

Humanism has been a powerful set of ideas. It is not a stretch to say it created both capitalism and democracy. And those values increased the power of the Industrial Revolution and enabled it to provide an ever- growing array of resources to enhance the value and enjoyment of life.

But even assuming that this idea of the central role of humanism is correct, one should ask: Are humanism (and democracy) pretty much necessary conditions for capitalism (and therefore for its benefits) to flourish?

Capitalism has not flourished in Russia (greed, yes, capitalism, no—greed flourishes everywhere under all economic systems). Capitalism also has not flourished in most other countries where authoritarian rule prevails. My guess is that to embrace capitalism requires the rulers to trust the people to make their own decisions— that is what competitive markets are about, and without competitive markets, capitalism is a sham.

Autocrats cannot trust people to make their own decisions because, if allowed to do so, the people might well throw out the autocrats. Thus one can hypothesize that democracy may be a prerequisite for capitalism, although history may show there have been some exceptions. (Maybe modern Singapore. Maybe Japan pre-1945. I think not China, although China uses some of the mechanisms of capitalism in selected ways.)

China may pose a challenge to the capitalism-democracy-humanism paradigm that I have outlined. At least it may do so at this time, having had a growing economy for 40 years while maintaining a large state-owned economy alongside the capitalist one, an autocratic state, and decidedly non-humanist social policies. Can China take the next economic steps and bring its people into the more affluent elites of the world while maintaining its strict government control? The official Chinese news organization has hailed a new science of "Sinomics" and China's rulers of course say it can be done. But Daron Acemoglu of MIT and James Robinson of Harvard, in their 2012 book, *Why Nations Fail*, argued convincingly that China could not remain autocratic and continue to succeed. Economist George Magnus of Oxford University, in his book *Red Flags: Why Xi's China Is In Jeopardy* (Yale University Press 2018) summarizes the question this way:

> "[Chinese President] Xi's intention is to show that an authoritarian, even dictatorial China can switch its economic agenda seamlessly away from high growth and malinvestment towards greater equality, a better environment, financial stability, OECD-type wealth status, and global technological leadership. … If it happened, China would be the first authoritarian country or dictatorship to do so."

The jury is still out—and I think it will remain out for quite a long time.

But regardless of whether Sinomics works as well as capitalism, capitalism, combined with democracy, has a moral basis that makes the system more than just something that works.

We should remember that America created democracy. People talk about Athens of 2500 years ago, but because so few people who lived in Athens were allowed to vote (maybe 12%), Athens was more an oligopoly than a democracy. England had its Magna Carta, giving the people some rights, in 1215, and it had fairly broad-based (but male-only) elections beginning in 1832, but until some time in the 20th century, the Crown kept a tight leash on British democracy. Only with the inauguration of George Washington in 1789 was the first national democracy actually born (but still with limited suffrage). And only America can truly defend the democratic values it created.

Materialism, Boom and Bust, and Inequality

The Industrial Revolution ushered in an era of unprecedented material advancement. Whereas the human standard of living had almost stagnated for over a thousand years, inventions like the steam engine, electricity, the light bulb, the internal combustion engine, indoor plumbing, etc. made great leaps forward. Food became more plentiful and took less labor to produce, humans captured energy from the ground and made it useful in ways that eclipsed animal energy. People could move from place to place faster, making trade more practical and thereby enhancing the diversity of available goods. From the beginning of the 19th century to the proliferation of central air conditioning in the 1960s, personal comfort and choice grew by leaps and bounds—for everyone, not only the wealthy.

By the beginning of the 20th century, the labor saved in the countryside caused people to move to cities. Governments in America adapted by instituting universal schooling through high school. And that led to an educated populace that could better run the machines and take advantage of the new technologies that kept on appearing. With the best-educated workforce, along with its abundant natural resources, America was able to outperform the world in production of the goods that consumers increasingly craved and could afford.

Did this materialism also lead to boom and bust cycles and to greater inequality as some people became rich and others did not?

Yes, to some extent. But one should remember that boom and bust and inequality had been staples of the world throughout history,

Boom and bust cycles existed even in agrarian societies, where the vagaries of the weather and pestilence caused famines and made food production inconsistent. When the crops failed, animals died, farmers could not pay their bills, banks failed, and even sovereigns defaulted on their debts.

And inequality had always existed. But for most of history, a very few people (royalty and rich landowners) were at the top and everyone else was down at the bottom, where they were fairly equal in their poverty. For the vast majority of people, life was "solitary, poor, nasty, brutish and short", in the words of 17th century philosopher Thomas Hobbes.

The mix of relative fortunes began to change in the 19th century, as the Industrial Revolution, combined with greater freedom to conduct business, enabled a middle class to create itself and enabled some commoners to rise economically to levels that theretofore had been possible only for royalty. Some writers have interpreted this as an increase in inequality, when in fact, for the first time, the huge middle of the population was becoming relatively well provided for.

In all eras, progress is decried as an insult to earlier values. And in most eras, there is nostalgia for a golden age that was better than the present. But in fact, except in times of war, ever since about 1750, progress has been steady, and life has become progressively longer and better—at least in the United States and most of Europe. And since the War of 1812 and excepting the Civil War years, the United States even has been comparatively blessed even in times of war because it is protected on two sides by great oceans and, since about 1836, on the other two sides by nations who have remained its allies.

To what extent has capitalism been responsible for this progress? Could it have occurred without capitalism? My answer is "no". One cannot do a scientific experiment to test what would have happened if the U.S. and Britain had adopted a socialist form of economics in 1850. However, the logic of history points strongly to capitalism having been a key both to the American spirit of entrepreneurship and to its success.

But even if capitalism has been instrumental in increasing material wellbeing, the materialism that accompanies it has been decried as soul-destroying. As Professor Muller has explained: The Greek philosopher Aristotle regarded commerce "not only as inimical to political virtue, but as a hazard to the moral well-being of the individual."

Professor Muller went on to discuss how materialism has been denigrated through the years:

> ➤ "[T]rade, in so far as it aims at making profits, is most reprehensible, since the desire for gain knows no bounds but reaches into the infinite." *The Mind and the Market*, pp. 5 and 8.

> ➤ "That trade was inimical to communal cohesion was a staple of the civic republican assumptions of early modern political thought." (p. 13)

> ➤ The most consistent worry of intellectuals, Professor Muller said, is that the success of materialism "would lead to a life filled with choices but devoid of meaning." (p. 395)

> ➤ 19th century German philosopher Hegel's "fear was that individuals might become mere playthings of the want-creating machine that was the market." (p. 396)

> "[20th century philosopher] Marcuse, more radically, saw the market as little more than a machine for want manipulation, at the expense of real happiness." (p. 396)

The list could go on. As Professor Muller concluded, "Every new revolution in consumption is greeted with the same warnings of impending doom." (p. 405)

That some individuals become prisoners of material desires cannot be denied. The questions are whether that condition is widespread and, if it is, what to do about it. I will leave those questions without answers. They are serious questions about the modern world, but I submit that they exist in all societies. I delight in my iPhone that allows me to communicate with the world and takes beautiful pictures but I care not for bling. I would not judge me better than the person who cares about both. Our inner lives and our relations with others may be rich or poor regardless.

Although capitalism may tend to encourage materialism, capitalism also helps the arts to flourish and thereby enriches people's spiritual lives. As French philosopher Voltaire said, "Abundance is the mother of the arts." An artist can suffer poverty in her attic for just so long. Her goal is to sell her books, paintings, operas, etc. in order to gain recognition and enjoy life. Being discretionary purchases, art is supported only when there are patrons with resources.

In the Middle Ages, art only flourished in churches and monasteries, where bishops and abbots encouraged a select few artists. And in some places, monarchs became patrons. The arts began to flourish more widely in commercial centers such as Venice and Amsterdam in the Renaissance, as some merchants became wealthy enough to be patrons.

But once the Industrial Revolution was under way, artists actually could originate without having designated patrons. They could (like other capitalists) rely on markets of relatively wealthy people who might find value in their paintings, sculptures and musical pieces. Markets like that produced modern art—from the Impressionists in the 1860s onward.

Although some art is revolutionary, it only flourishes if there are people who will pay for it.

CHAPTER 3

Capitalism's Difficulties

Some of Capitalism's Major Defects

Among capitalism's natural defects are:

➤ The price mechanism at the heart of capitalism does not take good account of what economists call "externalities".

➤ Capitalism does not tell us what we should do to assist those who lose out in the competitive process.

Capitalism and "Externalities"

Capitalism does not take good account of what economists call "externalities", meaning effects that are not of immediate concern to consumers when they make economic decisions. At the present time, climate change and air and water quality are the most important externalities that ordinary consumers logically do not take into account when they buy toothpaste and trash bags. That is because the costs of protecting the environment do not show up in ordinary pricing, unless government somehow forces businesses to bear a share of the costs—and one hopes, forces them to bear the costs somewhat in proportion to the environmental burdens that the particular business imposes. Such regulations induce the market to include environmental costs as well as the costs of production, marketing etc. in setting prices. If those environmental costs are in the prices that consumers pay, they will be part of consumers' decision-making that allocates resources and determines which goods and services will be popular.

There are many versions of mechanisms to make environmental costs a part of the costs that consumers pay. Regardless of what mechanisms, if any, one prefers, the fundamental generally accepted point is that without some form of government regulation/coercion, externalities like the environment do not sufficiently get taken into account by the forces that set prices—and therefore environmentally costly goods and services get bought more than they should be.

Winners and Non-Winners

Capitalism also naturally has winners and non-winners. Some people flourish, while other people do not. That is the nature of competition.

The theory of capitalism does not tell us what we should do about this problem. What, if anything, should society take from the winners? What, if anything, should society give to the less fortunate? Perhaps it is because the theory of capitalism tells us almost nothing about how to deal with these natural effects, the subject has become one of the most vexing in democratic capitalist societies. Of necessity, the answers are political ones.

My personal political preferences are that a wealthy nation like the U.S. should provide a safety net for those who need it. Though not part of the theory of capitalism, a safety net is necessary in order to sustain support for the benefits of capitalism in a democratic society and in order to be "fair"—though I admit that fairness is a subjective criterion that has little substance except personal preference.

But even though I think a better safety net is needed, one should not forget that in the U.S.:

I. The bottom half of the population is far better off than it was anywhere in the world at any time before capitalism.

2. The bottom half is far better off than it is in any place that does not have capitalism.

3. Personal economic resources are far less unequal than in any nation on earth before capitalism or have ever been in any nation that did not have capitalism.

(European democratic socialist countries are capitalist; they only have decided to divide the fruits of capitalism differently than America has. In the past, most such countries have had fairly homogeneous populations, which made it easier for them to share benefits.)

Capitalism's moral legitimacy requires, in my opinion, limiting the economic distance between winners and non-winners, either by what is being called "pre-distribution" or by redistribution. It appears that some affluent parts of American society reject that concept, though usually they clothe that rejection not as a moral rejection but as an acceptance of reality. That is, they assert that redistribution would reduce the level of economic growth that benefits everyone. Thus they claim that the well-meaning moral position that advocates redistribution is self-defeating.

Though there are pre-distribution and redistribution mechanisms that I agree are likely to be self-defeating, I believe it is demonstrable that some such mechanisms would not be self-defeating. The public policy task is to design policies that maximize equality while minimizing any negative impact on productivity and growth. There is no magic formula for doing this. But it can be done to a far greater extent than America is doing today.

Equality of Opportunity

Equality of opportunity is, to many of capitalism's defenders (including me) a necessary part of the system. Yet it is clear that in America today, as everywhere else in the world, people are not born with equal opportunities to succeed. They never have been.

People are born with unequal amounts of family money, with unequal amounts of parental understanding of their needs, and with unequal genetic make-ups. Therefore they manifestly do not begin with equal opportunities. From my point of view, making opportunity more equal is a critical point of public policy and a critical defense of capitalism's values.

But even if we level the opportunity of newborns as much as we can, we can never make everything equal, even at birth. Each human has traits and talents that are more or less unique. How good they are is a matter of luck.

Yet the Declaration of Independence says "all men are created equal" (it should have said "people" of course) and Americans have embraced that idea ever since. But what can it mean to say that all people are created equal when that is so manifestly not true in a literal sense?

I think it means that all people are equal in the eyes of the law and that the state should carry out that legal equality. No person should be given a preference by reason of status.

Equality also cannot mean that each person should lead exactly the same life as every other person. People self-differentiate, both due to accidents of birth and due to self-discovery. And that self-differentiation is respected—it is even encouraged—by American law and tradition. Therefore we should not expect—or even advocate—"equality of outcomes" because that presumes we all are the same, as manifestly we are not.

On the other hand, we never should say that a person has "got his/her just deserts in life", as some of capitalism's defenders on the right might say. There can be nothing that we call "just" when luck is so much of a determinant. (For a defense of the "just deserts" theory, see an essay by Harvard economist Greg Mankiw "Spreading the Wealth around: Reflections Inspired by Joe the Plumber". I think it is nonsense, but that is just my opinion.)

Another, similar rubric of conservative thought is that "The ability to enjoy the fruits of one's own labors is axiomatically a form of liberty," as Jonah Goldberg argued in the National Review in June 2019.

To Jonah Goldberg, any governmental action that detracts from a person's ability to enjoy the "fruits of one's own labor" is an assault on liberty. A tax therefore is an assault on liberty—and I suppose it is. But liberty is "axiomatically" restricted as soon as one is part of a society of more than one person. Merely saying that something (like taxation) restricts liberty is meaningless.

However, a serious question that advocates of capitalism need to address is: Can there be something we would call equality of opportunity even though we know that luck is unequal? The answer to this question is important because without something we can call equality of opportunity, we need to think seriously about outcomes—and that focus would lead us away from the mechanisms of the market and capitalism and toward a system in which elites decide what is good for the rest of us—and in which everyone subtly (or forcefully) would be pressed to conform to bureaucrats' idea of what people should be like.

I believe there can be a sufficient level of equality of opportunity that we need not address the equality of outcomes conundrum. My argument is as follows:

Not everyone has the opportunity to be Einstein or a basketball professional. Genetically, those are beyond almost everyone. But most people have sufficient genetic advantage to be able to live a successful life. The problem is that other circumstances of birth frequently prevent young people from achieving that potential. But if society works to redress those other accidents of birth, then there can be sufficient equality of opportunity that would permit society to feel that it has done a kind of practical moral justice. What the individual does with that moral justice is entirely separate.

(Yes, I am talking about "moral justice" even though I have not defined it and cannot define it—and even though not everyone will agree with the sense of moral justice that I am expressing. That is a limitation that I cannot see a way to avoid.)

America is not yet a society that has gone far enough to redress accidents of birth. There is a long way to go.

How far does society have to go in leveling the non-genetic playing field in order to achieve my notion of practical moral justice? That important question is beyond the scope of this more general discussion, but my book *The Education Solution* is about what America should do in order to make it possible for less affluent children to reach kindergarten as prepared as more affluent children. That would be an important beginning to creating equality of opportunity, and I think it is quite possible to achieve, if we have the political will to do so.

My main point here is that there can be a morally legitimate concept of equality of opportunity without equality of outcomes and that it can be moral for society to strive for equality of opportunity but not necessarily equality of outcomes, with a safety net for those whose outcomes turn out to be significantly deficient.

Getting comfortable with a level of equality of opportunity is critical to promoting progress because incentives to succeed are critical to human progress and greater prosperity for the vast majority. Making all economic outcomes equal would destroy an important source of incentive.

Not all incentives must be monetary—incentives can come in other forms, such as feelings of accomplishment or feelings of having helped other people. But we do need some kind of motivation to get up in the morning and contribute. If we have no motivation, progress will grind to a slow crawl, and everyone will suffer.

I also believe that people are happiest when they feel that they have contributed and that work is ennobling. Most successful people agree. They do not tend to retire; they tend to work until very late in their lives.

I count myself successful even though I had to close my most ambitious business, Sports Simulation, inc., in 2000. When we had to close, several of my employees said, "Boss, this was the best job I ever had." They said that not because I paid them so much—I could not afford to pay them lavishly— but because we had a common enterprise in which we all took pride. I had failed them, but their pride and understanding made that failure bearable. Even at the end, they said "boss" affectionately, and I have treasured that. I like to think we all were winners, despite our failure to achieve profitability.

Natural Monopolies, State Responsibilities, and Public Amenities

Capitalism has natural limitations as well as frailties that people take advantage of in the absence of good regulation.

Capitalism works well when there is a competitive market, but it does not work well without a competitive market. Situations without competitive markets include:

> ➢ natural monopolies" such as local providers of water and electricity,

> ➢ police and fire protection,

> ➢ some types of education,

> ➢ most roads, sewer systems, airports, passenger trains, and other public amenities.

In those situations, government usually attempts to create alternative competitive mechanisms. But often those attempts are not successful.

Regardless of the mechanism government uses to simulate competition, the political process and bribery (often subtle stuff that many people think is not bribery), graft, and general cronyism interfere. The quid pro quo need not be explicit for it to be effective. That is, alas, the nature of the world. Moreover, when the people at the top take liberties to enrich themselves, the rot quickly seeps down through the system, with many middle decision-makers declaring, "Well, everybody does it." The U.S. is not alone in having experienced that phenomenon, but some cultures are more prone to it than others.

Adam Smith understood very well that governments can be captured by producers who will use monopolies, tariffs, and tax systems for their own benefit. As stated by the Adam Smith Institute,

"the system is automatic only when there is free trade and competition. When governments grant subsidies or monopolies to favoured producers, or shelter them behind tariff walls, they can charge higher prices. . . .A further theme of *The Wealth Of Nations* is that competition and free exchange are under threat from the monopolies, tax preferences, controls, and other privileges that producers extract from the government authorities.

Smith also observed that a major defect of permitting such distortions from competitive market principles is that: "The poor suffer most from this, facing higher costs for the necessities that they rely on."

Crony capitalism is nothing new, nor are its natural effects. It is too bad that purported proponents of capitalism promote the kinds of privileges that capitalism's theoreticians have scorned going back to capitalism's earliest days. Crony capitalists use the rhetoric of capitalism to line their own pockets.

Nor is anticompetitive conduct limited to large companies or wealthy individuals. Adam Smith observed 250 years ago that whenever merchants gather, they seek to fix prices. The same often is true today. I recommend the clear and convincing talk by the late Princeton economics professor Alan Krueger at the Fed's Jackson Hole meeting on August 23, 2018 if you need evidence.

And I have witnessed merchants seeking to fix prices myself.

What about "Free Markets"?

Republicans almost uniformly embrace the idea of "free markets" as being the key to capitalism's benefits. But although the phrase "free markets" has a nice ring to it, it is a false mantra. The phrase has been used as much to *abuse* capitalism, as to support it. That is because in order for capitalism to work properly, government must establish rules for enforcing contracts, for preventing monopolies, and for preventing sellers not only from committing fraud, but also from abusing information asymmetries (they know their products better than you do). Without such rules, capitalism is a sham. It is not the capitalism that works in favor of the American people. But the free market mantra can be used (and has been used) as a reason to oppose any and all forms of regulation, no matter how beneficial on balance.

Peter Thiel is an unusually forthright tech billionaire. He says that capitalism and competition are opposites. Capitalism seeks profits but competition competes profits away. Competition, Thiel says, is for "losers". See Adam Tooze, Crashed (2018) at Kindle location 8826.

Because Thiel is correct that owners of capital seek to make monopoly profits wherever possible, we need strong antitrust laws, not free markets. More on antitrust in Chapter 7.

Greenspan's *Capitalism in America*

Former Federal Reserve Board Chairman Alan Greenspan contends in his book *Capitalism in America* that capitalism was responsible for the growth of the American economy in the 19th century. Even more, he contends that *laissez faire* capitalism and its lack of restraints on businesses—even business monopolies—were good for America, and he seems to mourn enactment of antitrust laws and just about every other restraint on business. (*Laissez faire* and "free markets" are two ways of saying about the same thing.)

Greenspan's contentions about *laissez faire* are, it seems to me, fairly typical of capitalism's defenders. As a consequence, they get fairly short shrift from a large part of the population, most especially younger Americans.

If capitalism is going to succeed in 21st century America, as I believe it can and should, it needs to have a softer side that protects consumers and protects workers who are laid off by technology or foreign competition—or indeed for any reason. Without such a softer side, capitalism will be the whipping boy for every form of populist, and their egalitarian rhetoric will prevail in the public arena.

There are at least a dozen other books, several of which are in this book's bibliography, that promote Greenspan's version of free market capitalism.

Defenders of capitalism, however, need to see its faults and dangers as well as its advantages and need to explain how to mitigate them.

Excessive Regulation in Support of Capitalism

The defenders of the free markets mantra respond to attacks like mine by saying that what they are doing is fighting back against unnecessary regulations that can choke off the benefits of capitalism. And the "free market" rhetoric, they say, is merely a popular shorthand.

It is true that regulations can become overbearing or excessive and thus can render capitalism less efficient. It also is true that the advocates of additional regulation (usually including many Democrats) rarely recognize the need to eliminate ineffective or overbearing regulation. And it even is true that regulation is used to prevent competition as well as to permit dominant companies to engage in "regulatory capture", whereby they befriend the regulators to such an extent that they get favored treatment. These are natural hazards.

We do have many laws and regulations that we would be better off without. But both sides should recognize that the issues rarely are clear-cut, and that in most cases, the best solution is a balancing of interests.

It is natural that political battles are fought about externalities, about consumer protection, about taxation, and about safety net issues. There are natural tradeoffs in each of these areas. And the basic theory of capitalism does not determine where the lines should be drawn. It would be better, however, if logic rather than slogans determined where to draw the lines.

Some questions about each area illustrate the needed logic:

> Preventing emissions of greenhouse gasses has a clear cost in the extra expenses of factories and in people's freedom to move around and to live as they might like. How much productivity and freedom should society give up today in order to protect future generations?

> How detailed and burdensome should building regulations be in order to protect people from damage?

> How detailed should consumer disclosure rules be before they become self-defeating or impose excessive costs on the products in question?

> What or how much should people be entitled to for no cost before we conclude that the damage to their incentives to work and be otherwise productive are too compromised or that the cost to society is greater than the benefit?

> At what point, if any, does taxation of the affluent cause them to reduce their efforts?

> What kinds of tax incentives, if any, does capital need to be given to invest?

People reasonably can differ as to how to answer these questions—and people in fact do differ strongly about them. But they are the kinds of questions that voters and consumers have to answer.

A healthy democratic capitalist system debates the merits of specific regulations vigorously in an effort to keep or to institute those that are needed to protect people, the market, and future generations, and to eliminate or to not adopt regulations that foster inefficiency without providing sufficient benefits. Policy needs to focus better on these dichotomies—and that begins by admitting that they are real.

Business Aggregates versus Individual Workers

Early in the 19th century, limited liability companies and the advent of historically freer economic laws made it possible for merchants to join together to expand their businesses. Such amalgamated businesses have natural advantages of many types. Many of those advantages were key to expanding the Industrial Revolution. But one of the advantages that larger business aggregates have is in bargaining with workers. Those advantages gradually led governments to permit employees to band together in industrial unions that sought to improve workers' bargaining power. The struggle was mighty, with the courts often siding with employers and employers decrying the worker-monopolists. But gradually, after over a century of progress, trade unions became legally accepted in the U.S. and in most of Europe by the first half of the 20th century.

One can say that trade unions are a necessary balance to the ability of businesses to form limited liability companies and, thereby, to raise capital and increase their geographic and financial scope. In evaluating that last sentence, one should recognize that the limited liability company and the freedom to form large business aggregates were legislative accomplishments of capitalism's advocates—not aspects of business that preceded capitalism. They are important parts of what made capitalism successful. Thus trade unions can be seen as an appropriate balancing mechanism—indeed, in some settings, trade unions might be seen almost as a necessary part of capitalism itself.

Thus by the end of WWII, trade unions were a part of industrial life both in the U.S. and throughout Europe. Entire industries often had a single union that represented its employees, and contract bargaining in those industries became events of national importance. Strikes in major industries triggered privation for thousands of workers, including many whose jobs in supplier businesses came to a halt even though they were not part of the bargaining. The strikes also caused shortages for many consumers. The height of this business/union domination of American economic life came in the 1950s, but though in decline, continued in the 1960s and 1970s.

But then things changed. The comparative benefits and detriments of the changes are debatable. I do not propose to resolve them. The issues that change created cry out for resolution, but although a satisfactory resolution would make a better capitalism, the basic value of capitalism does not depend on that resolution.

My main points here are (1) that there was a time that trade unions were an integral part of American capitalism, and (2) that the changes were caused at least in part by changes in the nature of work and of businesses, not only by changes in the American political climate.

How the Middle Class Has Fared Economically since 1970

Today, by contrast with, say, 1970, the middle class is not composed of unionized workers. Instead, it is composed largely of better-educated people in two-worker families. And in economic terms, those middle class families are better off today than the middle class families of the 1970 era. Here are the data on incomes in inflation-adjusted dollars from the official website census.gov (Table H-3). The most recent data are from 2017. (I should note that these are "mean" or average numbers, and therefore that the first and fifth quintiles are not reliable indications of progress or lack of progress by the median families in those quintiles.)

Year	First Quintile	Second Quintile	Third Quintile	Fourth Quintile	Fifth Quintile
1970	11,253	30,484	49,089	69,193	122,498
1980	12,242	30,468	50,277	74,070	132,064
1990	13,072	32,889	54,325	81,907	158,951
2000	14,498	36,201	60,285	93,716	203,081
2010	12,387	32,148	55,397	88,872	190,856
2017	13,258	35,401	61,564	99,030	221,846

Although all quintiles appear better off today than in 1970, the contrast between the meager progress made by the second quintile compared with the fourth quintile is striking. Inequality has increased.

It also is striking that the income of all quintiles went down in the 2000 to 2010 period due to the Great Recession. And although as of 2017, the third and fourth quintiles had recovered to above their highs in 2000, the second quintile had not recovered completely, even though it was far better off than it had been in 2010.

We also see that, contrary to much popular belief, the 1970s were not a good period for the middle class, largely because of inflation that robbed their incomes of spending power.

The 1990s were a statistical golden age for the middle class. I once asked an economist friend who had been in the Clinton Administration how they had accomplished that. He said he didn't know, but added Puckishly that they took "full credit for it".

I conclude that the macro events, such as economic growth, inflation, and the Great Recession, rather than political policies, tend to dominate the middle class economic progress story. Comparatively, adjustments of detailed policies seem to make less difference.

(I also should note that the Census Bureau data are not the only way to look at the progress or lack thereof of the middle class economically. The Congressional Budget Office (CBO) also maintains data—and its data include many kinds of government transfers and adjust for income taxes paid. The CBO data tend to make the middle class look like it has made more progress than the Census Bureau data show. I have used the Census Bureau data because they are the most frequently used.)

The Decline of Industrial Unions In America

In the immediate post-WWII period, American manufacturing was globally dominant vis-à-vis factories and populations in Europe and Asia that had been destroyed in the War. By the 1970s, however, competition in many businesses became international in scope, as foreign nations recovered. And this globalized workforce has continued to grow and to compete with American workers. As a consequence, many high-cost U.S. businesses have failed or contracted, and many functions have been outsourced to less expensive jurisdictions. That has eroded the potential gains that labor unions can make. This is true in Europe as well as in the U.S. Trade unions remain stronger in Europe, but over the last 20 years, their power has diminished considerably. See Donald Sassoon, *The Anxious Triumph* at p. 516.

In addition to external competitive factors, after the advent of central air conditioning in the 1960s, much of American manufacturing migrated from the unionized north to the non-union south in order to take advantage of lower employee costs. Many southern states had and have laws that are not union-friendly.

It is important as well that the nature of work began to change. Whereas in the typical industrial process, many workers did basically the same job and were interchangeable, in the new economy, jobs have tended to be more differentiated. And it became less appropriate for people with highly differentiated jobs (and highly differentiated pay) to bargain together. Increased efficiency also led to smaller numbers of workers being able to produce larger amounts of goods. All these factors led to the gradual decline of industrial union membership.

By the 21st century, industrial labor unions have become a relatively minor factor in the protection of American workers. That has left a void in the worker-employer balance that 20th century capitalism had struck. Both so-called socialists and so-called populists are seeking to fill that void. And that void also has contributed to anti-capitalist sentiment.

To fill that void in a way that gives workers better bargaining power while enabling large employers to continue to compete and succeed seems like a difficult problem that needs to be addressed. I will discuss it a bit more in Chapter 6 on "Corporate Governance". I confess that I do not have a good universal answer.

But lest one become too enamored of the days of Big Labor as a solution, picture what happened in a major strike. I witnessed one.

As an associate lawyer at Ford's outside counsel, I was assigned as part of a team to write some of the Ford-UAW contract in 1967.The old contract expired (fittingly, I guess) on Labor Day. So that was when the strike began.

The office Ford gave us at their headquarters in Dearborn faced the giant River Rouge plant, the largest manufacturing facility in the world. It ran three shifts a day and belched a constant stream of smoke into the Michigan sky. But slowly the plant grew silent and static. Nothing moved for six weeks, while Ford and the UAW wrestled about how to divvy up the pie of corporate cashflow. In the end, neither side got what it wanted.

Meanwhile, the giant plant baked in the September sun and September turned into October. Ford produced no cars and lost market share to GM (which did not have a strike because the UAW— sensibly— used a divide and conquer bargaining strategy) and the Ford workers received no wages for six long weeks. The union's strike fund helped some, but the hardships were terrible—and even worse for some employees of Ford's suppliers who were not on strike.

There were many big strikes in those days. As a society, we need to learn a better way to provide fairness to workers than to try to go back to the labor strife of the 1950s and 1960s.

One also might observe that the companies that employees now rate the best to work for often are not unionized. Some are, but a majority of the top 25 large companies ranked favorably by their employees are not primarily unionized.

What appears to make a bigger difference than unionization is that the company have a vision that exalts their employees as key to their success. Thus, Trader Joe's, a food discounter, is number one, and if you shop in one of their stores, you can see that their employees are different. The same is true of Costco (number four) and Wegman's (number nineteen).

Southwest Airlines is number two, and it is unionized. But if you fly Southwest, you can see the difference, as you can when you fly Jet Blue, which is number eleven.

Google and Apple are there, too (six and sixteen). They pay well and they recognize that their real assets ride up and down in the elevator.

More on company ethos will be in Chapter 6 on Corporate Governance. It is a subject that has received too little attention, even though it has a big impact on the lives of both workers and consumers.

Is the Problem Globalization?

Could reduced globalization help to fix the problem? No. Globalization—that is, global competition—is a fact. It will not go away. It is, in effect, the only game in town. The question is how you are going to play it. Are you going to try to make things better for everybody, including yourself? Or are you going to try to beggar your neighbor for your own benefit?

Yes, global competition has cost some American jobs and it will cost additional jobs in the future. But it also has created American jobs and it will create more American jobs in the future.

Do some nations not "play fair" in this competition? Yes, some nations try not to play fair. The questions are whether they succeed by doing that and, if so, how to respond to that?

If we pay attention to how global trade and investment actually work, the answers are quite simple because in practical terms, no one can gain a permanent advantage by ignoring the rules. There is, instead, a set of automatic stabilizers that removes the apparent advantage from artificially depressing one's currency or using the state to subsidize particular companies or industries—or even using tariffs as a weapon.

It takes faith and persistence to act on these understandings. But doing so is to the long-term benefit of the nations that do. That is because trade is not a zero sum game. It enlarges the opportunity for everyone, and using global or regional alliances to smooth the way and to promote trade in the long run enlarges the economic pie for all. Putin's (and Trump's) beggar-thy-neighbor nationalistic policies may appear to benefit their nations in the short term, but in the long term, they detract from their nations' economic wellbeing.

The theory of capitalism tells us that—and it works. The missing piece in America is to provide sufficient protections for people whose jobs are eliminated, whether by trade, technology or other reasons. We need not ask the reason for job loss. We should protect workers who lose their jobs in all cases. The new jobs that get created often are better jobs, and the additional taxes those new jobs generate can pay for the safety net and retraining that the temporary non-winners need.

*"It is imperative
that we create a government
that works for all and not just the few."*

- Bernie Sanders

CHAPTER 4

Is Socialism Better? Whose Socialism?

European Democratic Socialism

What should we say here about European democratic socialism? Is it socialism or is it capitalism or is it something else? And is that European formulation a different humanistic formulation whose success (or failure) threatens capitalism?

My answer is that European democratic socialism, as practiced in most European nations, is merely a variant of democratic market capitalism that seeks to redress some of capitalism's natural defects by providing better safety nets for people who get left behind. Most of the means of production are in private hands, and most prices are set by the market, although EU subsidies for agriculture and a few other things violate capitalism's principles, just as many American subsidies do.

Finance for the means of production, similarly, is a market function rather than being provided by government in most European countries. On those occasions that European nations have tried to nationalize the banking business, it has led to failure. This was the case when France nationalized its major banks after World War II and when France and Belgium cooperated to found a bank called Dexia that failed in 2011. The Austrian experience has been similar.

Whether the broad safety net provided by many European nations has drawbacks and whether it could work effectively in America are widely debated questions. But the reasonable range of answers to those questions does not contradict the value of the basic market mechanisms of capitalism.

A July 7, 2019 New York Times op-ed discussed the "public option" for many types of amenities, including public parks (I grew up in the public parks of the Bronx), public swimming pools (ditto), public libraries (ditto), public schools, public colleges, the post office, public health, public internet access, perhaps a public banking access (which I have advocated in a limited, electronic-only form via the Federal Reserve Banks), and calls for more such public access alternatives.

These types of public amenities are not inconsistent with capitalism. They have flourished alongside capitalism for substantially all of American history, and they can be expanded, as the op-ed advocated.

Government can do many useful things while maintaining capitalism as its form of economic governance.

Socialism and Bernie Sanders

Today's attacks on capitalism frequently are summarized as a preference for "socialism"—a political term that has been championed in the U.S. by Senator Bernie Sanders. Therefore I have asked myself, "What is this socialism that Bernie Sanders advocates and that is so attractive to, especially, young people?" And is that socialism antithetical to capitalism?

Until about August 2019, I had concluded that Sanders' socialism is not socialism as an economist previously would have understood the term. Indeed, it strongly appeared that Sanders' socialism was not antithetical to or inconsistent with capitalism. He was a capitalist who would like better government controls and a better safety net. He refused, as far as I can tell, to admit that he was a capitalist, but his definition of socialism identified him as a capitalist who advocates that the system be run less in the interests of the moneyed classes.

Here are excerpts from a Time Magazine report of what appears to have been a typical 2018 Sanders speech:

> When I use the word socialist—and I know some people aren't comfortable about it—I'm saying that it is imperative,' Sanders said, that we 'create a government that works for all and not just the few.'
>
> '**I don't believe government** should **own the means of production**, but I do believe that the middle class and the working families who produce the wealth of America deserve a fair deal,' he said. [Emphasis added by ML.]

Sanders' principal concrete proposals were Medicare for all, free college education, and a higher minimum wage. These were hardly either revolutionary or anti-capitalist sentiments. One might agree with them or disagree with them, but they all were within the economic and social mainstream of American thought for the last 70 years. Therefore, in my opinion, Bernie Sanders was not really a socialist.

If Sanders was not a socialist, why did he call himself a socialist, and why was the rest of the American political world willing to do so as well? The reason seems to be that Americans on the right have derided all forms of safety net programs as "socialist", at least since the days of FDR, when they derided things like Social Security as socialist. Sanders has been happy to identify with that legacy because FDR retains people's respect and because it separated him from other "liberal" or "progressive" politicians who may espouse essentially the same things that he did.

The campaign for the 2020 nomination has, however, driven many of the Democratic candidates leftward. Sanders now appears to be trying to catch up with his supporters by moving further left than his formerly soft socialism. This is especially evident in his embrace of a radical form of "Green New Deal" under which the government would undertake a $16 trillion program to substantially eliminate emission of greenhouse gases in a very few years.

That program would entail fundamental changes in the American system of government, including greater control over citizens' lives. Bernie Sanders, therefore, is now a socialist for real. Parts of his 2020 program could destroy some of the benefits of capitalism and would force many Americans to remake the way they live.

Liberals are wary of imposing their own way of living on others. The new Sanders program, like other forms of autocracy, has no such restraint. Although the objective of reducing emissions is embraced by all Democratic politicians that I have heard, the Green New Deal is reminiscent of Republican presidential nominee Barry Goldwater's 1964 absolutist assertion that "extremism in support of liberty is no vice; moderation in pursuit of justice is no virtue." As so often, the right and the left seem alike in their certainty that they know best.

The "Democratic Socialists of America"

The Democratic Socialists of America (DSA) are socialists. They advocate that the government should own the means of production and that all medicine should be socialized (not merely a single payer Medicare-like system). The DSA website says:

"The Democratic Socialists of America (DSA) is the largest socialist organization in the United States. We believe that working people should run both the economy and society democratically to meet human needs, not to make profits for a few. We are a political and activist organization, not a party; through campus and community-based chapters, DSA members use a variety of tactics, from legislative to direct action, to fight for reforms that empower working people."

The DSA is an anti-capitalist movement that is hard to distinguish from what used to be called Communism. The DSA and its adherents would repudiate capitalist principles and its benefits in favor of businesses run by the state.

The DSA and its adherents (of which Alexandria Ocasio-Cortez (AOC) apparently is one) are a relatively small group at this time, but their use of the term socialism to describe something different from what Bernie Sanders has meant is likely to confuse the electorate. That confusion could be important.

And that confusion cannot be cured by me having another Humpty Dumpty moment. That would not alter what the electorate think socialism means.

Regardless of what you call it, AOC's rhetoric is anti-capitalist. In March 2019, she opined that "Capitalism is an ideology of capital—-the most important thing is the concentration of capital and to seek and maximize profit. And that comes at any cost to people and to the environment, so to me capitalism is irredeemable."

But sometimes AOC's rhetoric softens: She has said she doesn't think all parts of capitalism should be abandoned, "we're reckoning with the consequences of putting profit above everything else in society. And what that means is people can't afford to live. For me, it's a question of priorities and right now I don't think our model is sustainable."

Regardless of exactly what she means, her rhetoric and popularity are pushing Sanders and the Democratic Party leftward.

And whereas capitalism trusts the people to make their own decisions through the market, the DSA would dictate the results because they know best.

Taking a historical point of view, perhaps the attraction of socialism is best understood in the context of an assumption that the sum of goods and services (and therefore the sum of all standards of living) is relatively fixed. If it is fixed, then what one person has takes away from what each other person may have. This is an idea (held, among others, by the Catholic Church for centuries) that goes back over a thousand years:

> "Since the material wealth of humanity was assumed to be more or less fixed, the gain of some could only be conceived as a loss to others.

> "Profits from trade were therefore regarded as morally illegitimate." (*The Mind and the Market*, p. 5)

Thus, if global assets are fixed, then the struggle to allocate them fairly is urgent. But if the fixed assets view of the world is untrue (as the history of the last 250 years amply proves), then the division is less important than that at least some modicum is available to everyone—and that the sum continues to grow so that the defined minimum modicum to which all are entitled can grow as well.

As I said earlier, I conclude that the macro events, such as economic growth, inflation, and the Great Recession, rather than political policies, tend to dominate the middle class economic progress story. Comparatively, adjustments of detailed policies seem to make less difference.

Marx and his followers contended that "socialism would maintain the productivity of capitalism without its distributional inequalities and its moral blemishes.")The Mind and the Market, p. 391) But a review of economic history in countries that have followed the socialist (public ownership of the means of production) model strongly suggests that socialism does not maintain the productivity of capitalism and that it develops its own distributional inequalities because so often it is accompanied by authoritarian rule.

Indeed it appears that capitalism even can be the best cure for environmental pollution. "What's Behind the World's Biggest Climate Victory? Capitalism," says a Bloomberg.com headline. And the story explains how capitalism, by driving down costs, has made wind and solar less-cost alternatives to oil and coal for producing electricity.

By 2050, the story estimates, the U.S. will get substantially all of its electricity from renewable sources, even without any additional governmental action to require it. The magic is the market.

Socialism's Defects

It would be fairly easy to describe socialism's defects. But bashing socialism will not, I think, persuade young Americans that capitalism is preferable. What they need to know is that capitalism is moral, that it works, and that its defects can be remediated within its basic framework.

My criticisms of the young advocates of socialism such as AOC also may be taken amiss by young Americans as an older person (a white male, at that) telling them they are too young to know what is right.

Can What and Old Guy Says Be Relevant?

How can I assure young Americans that I respect them and their opinions? I will try a personal story.

When I was 29, I got an assignment to do the legal work for a small Caribbean airline to buy two used Boeing 707 jets from the Australian airline QANTAS. The financing for the jets fell apart on a Friday morning, when the pilots already were in Australia to fly the planes to the West Indies. The investment banker I was working with, also 29 years old, talked Boeing into providing financing for a temporary 60 days.

I was at home—in a pre-cell-phone era—on Friday evening when he called me to say we had to close the deal the next day. I called the Boeing lawyers, who told me they needed a legal opinion regarding ownership of the planes. I could not give that opinion because it was governed by the law of the airline's domicile in the West Indies. Somehow, I found the client's general counsel at home and asked if he could give the opinion. He said he could. But then Boeing wanted my back-up opinion that I had no reason to doubt the general counsel's opinion. I was an associate and not permitted to sign opinions, so I had to get a partner to work with me.

Obstacles kept getting put in our way, including finding that for tax reasons we could not close the deal in New York, where my office was—so I had to borrow an office outside New York. But with cooperation from people in Australia, the West Indies, New York and Seattle, we closed the deal in a borrowed office in Connecticut on Saturday and the planes flew out from Australia. I wrote the entire deal on one sheet of legal paper—a document that today would take perhaps thirty pages—and typed it myself.

My client never got the permanent financing, but the planes flew on that 60-day note that Boeing renewed every two months for almost a decade.

I tell this story because if I had been more experienced, I might have said that the Friday night demand to close on Saturday was impossible to meet. Being in my 20's—and the investment banker also being in his 20's—we saw possibilities that greater experience might have hidden from us.

CHAPTER 5

A Thought Experiment— Analyzing an Important Social Problem as an Example

Most of the problems that public policy makers deal with are complex. Perhaps it will be useful to engage in a thought experiment about one of America's most important and intractable public policy issues in order to see the kind of thinking that it may require. Unfortunately, our thought experiment will not resolve the issue, but maybe it will help us to understand how we might move forward—and how public money can be employed in ways that are entirely consistent with capitalism and its principles.

As our example, let's take the large disparity between economic groups in their success in education. I am on record as favoring a large public investment in early childhood education, including education of young parents, so that less affluent children can enter kindergarten just as prepared as their peers from more affluent backgrounds.

But there are other good ideas—and my idea may not be sufficient by itself, even if it is a correct idea.

I have chosen the education problem for our thought experiment because almost no one denies that the problem exists. The questions are what causes it and what to do about it.

The problem is particularly acute in the black neighborhoods of inner cities. And I will use New York and its suburbs for purposes of analysis just because it is the area where I grew up and lived most of my life.

The problem in New York has become so bad that very few black students are able to qualify for the elite public schools where admission is based on academic tests. The top high school is Stuyvesant, in lower Manhattan. In the 2019 tests, only 7 of 895 places went to black students. Bronx High School of Science invited only 12 black students out of a total of 803. In both cases, the numbers of black students have been dwindling for many years. Brooklyn Tech does a little better at 95 black invitees out of 1825, but considering the demography of Brooklyn, that is still a terrible result.

Whereas Stuyvesant made only 7 offers to black students, it made 33 to Hispanic students, 194 to white students, and 587 to Asian-American students. Although they received more than 80% of the offers, Asian- American students make up only about 15 percent of the total public school system.

I am not being critical of the current system, nor do I propose how to redress these imbalances. My point in outlining them is only to emphasize how extreme the imbalances have become.

The long-term solution—and there may be no good short-term solution—has to be to provide better educational opportunity to the black children of New York before they get to high school.

After that simple statement (duh!) the problem gets complicated because housing is seen as related to the quality of schooling—and the concentration of black students in particular areas is seen as one of the impediments to providing better educational opportunities. So where does a policy-maker begin? With housing? With new schools? With improving old schools? And if any one of those is the answer, how should it be done?

Again, my purpose here is not offer definitive answers. It is to analyze the problems and to show how different kinds of thinking might lead to different kinds of solutions—and different short-run public costs. (Long- run, a successful solution should pay for itself.)

Some thoughtful people, including Senator Elizabeth Warren, think the housing part of the puzzle is key. Senator Warren advocates building subsidized affordable housing outside New York City, in places where the schools are very good, and making it possible for families from the ghettos of the City to move into those apartments. There is evidence to back up Senator Warren's proposal in that inner city black students who have been able to attend largely white and Asian suburban schools have performed substantially better than they had performed in the ghetto schools from which they came. And black students in integrated schools perform better in general.

Senator Warren's thinking is an example of top-down thinking, where the elite decides what is good for a class of people and implements that using public money. A more capitalist (classically liberal) approach would say that the government should subsidize the people (through housing vouchers, for example) and let them decide where they wanted to live, now that they have greater means. Both these ways of approaching the education problem as a housing problem, however, have inherent difficulties that are not related to the different ways that they are justified. Both founder on the realities of suburban New York (which are similar to the realities of many other suburban areas).

The voluntary solution that gives people vouchers will not get them into the wealthy suburbs because the amount of money is not enough and there is little rental housing. The vouchers may (and should) improve their lives, but the vouchers are unlikely to make as big an impact on their children's education as advocates might hope. (Vouchers may be a sensible policy nevertheless.)

The solution that would put affordable housing in wealthy areas founders because it can accommodate only a relative few families, and even those few families are not wanted by the communities where they are to be planted. Therefore the members of those families likely will naturally feel different from the wealthier and better-educated families of the communities where they are planted. And for the children, that difference may translate into feelings of inferiority and anger.

My guess is that trying to solve the educational problem by diagnosing it as a housing problem will fail regardless of whether one tries the top- down or the bottom-up version. (Creating new segregated school districts, on the other hand, should not be permitted. Doing that would compound the problem.)

If the problem is education, my guess is that society must tackle the education problem, not try to make education better by focusing on something that may be related. But even though the housing solution probably is not a solution, that does not mean that the problem is the teachers or the schools alone.

Many kinds of data and observations suggest that the culture of the ghetto is a major part of the problem. However, we cannot just tell the ghetto to change. It is the way it is for many reasons, most of which are difficult to change.

One of the instincts that capitalists have is to try to provide some choices for people so that they can use market concepts to decide what is the best way to make improvements. In current education, charter schools are the principal way to do that, and there are many charter schools in New York City that have aimed to provide just that: a choice for parents and children to make as to the style of education they want.

My point is not that charter schools are better than regular public schools but that giving parents and students a choice will allow them to determine what education will be like in the future.

Some people, however, are concerned that most charter schools are not unionized. For them, that makes charter schools less desirable and, in a way, unfair competition. They also say that because a student has to elect to attend a charter school, charter schools tend to be elitist. And some also say that charter schools attempt to make students abandon their natural cultures in favor of becoming "whiter".

My response is that kids come first. If we want to offer better education and parents and students select charter schools, their decisions should be respected, and charter schools should be permitted to grow along with the demand.

But charter schools may not be the only successful approach.

On Manhattan's West Side and in Brooklyn's Park Slope area, there are new, parent-led experiments about to take place beginning in September 2019, where, within Districts 3 and 15, integration will be accomplished via a targeted lottery system in the junior high schools. The City approved the experiment, but the impetus and design came from the parents.

Some parents in the affected districts—particularly some white parents—are concerned that the schools their early teens attend will not be as good under the new system. Advocates point to evidence that students get a better education in integrated schools.

The designers of the experiment know there are risks. But the excellent thing is that the local people have created the design, which in both cases was facilitated by school districts that already had both wealthy and poor areas within their existing boundaries. That the experimental system applies only within existing boundaries may save it from serious legal threats based on the system's effective use of racial quotas.

My hope is that the experiment will be evaluated by well-designed academic studies that may tell the world what parts of this experiment work and what parts do not. Maybe by 2025 or so we will really know something. If this experiment does not work well, that will be a setback to many theories of how to attack the problem. If it is successful, then redrawing school district maps and using lotteries may become a useful way to deal with the issues in many areas. And then the housing questions will come into play once again.

The Benefits of Black Male Teachers

The issues regarding inner city education can become even more socially complex if we are willing to ask the really hard questions. About the hardest that I know of stems from data that show that black boys learn better when they have at least some teachers who are high-achieving black males. But there is a shortage of high-achieving black males who want to be teachers. And the reason for that appears to be that high-achieving black males are relatively scarce to begin with, and they are offered higher paying jobs in the private sector or in other parts of government service. Therefore, they need to be offered higher compensation to be attracted into teaching.

Let's say that schools cannot discriminate in favor of a category that is based both on gender and on race. But could a major foundation offer such teachers a summer "fellowship" of, say, $20,000 each? Would that be legal? Would it be desirable?

Looked at in the context of what attracting more black male teachers could accomplish, the cost could well be worth it. Indeed, the cost could pay for itself in the benefits to society by reducing criminal justice costs, reducing long-run safety net costs, and increasing earnings of black men so that they also would pay more taxes. See "Appendix D" at my website the-education-solution.com for an example of how such expenditures can more than pay for themselves over a number of years.

But the question of principle remains. Could we justify the discrimination? We could make this question even more acute if we were to posit that the benefits to male black students only accrue if the black male teachers are hetero. There is no data to that effect; I do not think the question has been studied. But as a thought experiment, we might add that additional aspect of discrimination.

Why do I pose these difficult questions? Because if we want to improve the educational results for inner city children—and particularly for boys, who perform more poorly than girls—then we have to be willing to learn what the boys need, and, if we can, to deliver what they need.

But suppose we do not like what they need?

There are unlikely to be simple answers to hard questions. And when a question has been hanging around for many decades without having an answer that succeeds, chances are that we have been looking for the wrong kind of answers.

"Liberalism loves sympathy,
suspects rage
and detests cruelty."
- David Brooks

CHAPTER 6

Corporate Governance

"Corporate governance" sounds like an esoteric subject that ordinary people don't have to pay attention to. But it is an important aspect of the 'plumbing" that makes any modern economic system work—or not work—regardless of whether it is a capitalist system or something else. Who appoints/elects the people who run business enterprises and the laws that govern the standards that they must apply can make a crucial difference in the effectiveness and the impacts of the enterprises.

In America, shareholders elect a board of directors that is in charge of the business of the corporation, and the board of directors designates officers who run the corporation's business day to day. The corporation laws typically just say that. They do not tell the officers how to run their businesses.

Both the directors and the officers owe their duties to the corporation, and those duties include diligence, loyalty and disclosure of conflicts of interests.

Shareholder corporate democracy is far from perfect, but it puts selecting management in the hands of owners. When a company is owned by the state, on the other hand, the people who run the state decide who should run the companies. And in some nations, such as Russia, lip service is paid to private ownership, but in practice, the state calls the tune.

Senator Elizabeth Warren is one of many advocates for a change in corporate governance whereby corporate boards would be required to have representatives of various "stakeholders" and the board as a whole would have responsibilities to those various stakeholders, including, most prominently, workers. Her proposal is called the Accountable Capitalism Act.

The U.K. study called "Prosperity and Justice" that I will discuss in Chapter 9 makes a similar recommendation. And her proposal to mandate employees on boards of directors is consistent with the rules of some northern European countries. This is not a new or radical idea globally.

I contend, however, that the traditional view in American corporate law is better: A corporate board that is required by law to serve many masters almost of necessity will be a corporate board whose business will not compete as actively in the marketplace as one that serves a single master— the corporate enterprise that they manage. Successful corporate boards do take account of employee, customer and other interests in order for their corporation to succeed, but legal requirements to consider them all would be quite different from considerations based on benefit to the business.

As I outlined earlier, some successful corporations adopt an ethos that includes the welfare of their employees. Trader Joe's, Southwest Airlines and Wegman's, for example, are legendary for their focus on employees and for the excellent results that focus brings for their customers. The nexus between employees who are happy to work where they work and excellent customer experiences is inescapable. Unhappy employees tend to be surly and aloof, and customers see that immediately.

The employee focus appears to be difficult to maintain as companies get bigger. Southwest Airlines is an example. Although it was founded with an employee focus, in recent years it has nevertheless experienced strained labor relations as it has grown from a regional airline into a national competitor.

There also are some companies that emphasize their loyalty to their customers' needs. H.E.B., a Texas grocer, provided free bottled water to its Houston customers when flooding had made municipal water unhealthy. The shopping experience at H.E.B. is enjoyable and the prices are competitive.

Yet there do appear to be managements that are intent only on financial engineering and fancy marketing ideas. My take, however, is that such managements do not last long. "Chainsaw Al" Dunlap, who was famous for cutting staff and other expenses in the 1990s, never really had a success, and he never was welcome anywhere for very long.

Although there is much rhetoric to the contrary, the data show that the stock market values long-term thinking and customer satisfaction. But that Trader Joe's, H.E.B. and Wegman's are not publicly owned may suggest that it is easier for a privately owned company to adopt an unusually pro-worker or pro-customer ethos. And the success of companies like Blackstone and KKR that take companies private, burnish their business models, and take them public again also may attest to shortcomings of the public ownership model.

Does the Delaware Corporation Model Need Change?

There are good reasons to ask whether the Delaware Law corporate governance model could be improved upon. I have wondered about that myself ever since I began writing about the subject in about 1970. That I have not found a better solution does not mean there is none. I will keep searching.

The stylized dance that has become the fixing of CEO compensation over the last 40 years is indicative that the system needs improvement. The following is a description of that dance by an investment professional:

"[A]nyone who has sat in on a board discussion of the CEO's salary, as I have, knows that it isn't "the market" evaluating the CEO. It is a form of subtle, or accidental, cronyism—something that the fundamental theory of perfect markets disallows.

What happens is that the board hires a consulting firm to create a matrix of executive pay in the same or similar industry in comparable geographic locations. The matrix includes average, high, and low levels of compensation among those the consulting firm surveyed.

Then the board uses that to discuss the CEO's compensation. Of course, it doesn't want to insult the CEO (unless the board actually wants to get rid of her) by calling her performance only average or less than average. So they choose a compensation level in the above average range. And of course, some of the board members are CEOs themselves.

This process inevitably causes a spiraling of CEO pay – which is what has happened."

Maybe Senator Warren's proposal makes sense.

Republicans, however, seem to give the back of their hand to Sen. Warren's proposed statute. See Wall Street Journal op-eds such as the op-ed that concludes:

"History teaches that if we want to be prosperous and free, within the rule of law, we must let private interests create wealth and reap the rewards. Only after wealth has been created should we debate the costs and benefits of re-distributing it to our desired social ends."

That is typical free market hogwash, in my opinion, and people who are concerned about inequality will pay no attention to it. Warren's proposal deserves to be taken seriously because some reforms are needed, even though I think Warren's proposal's adoption would be ruinous and therefore I advocate rejecting it, as I will explain.

The current push that corporate boards should owe duties to many stakeholders seems to derive from the mistaken idea that corporate boards are responsible only to stockholders' short-term interests and therefore ignore the long-term health of the corporation. That idea seems to derive from a famous speech by University of Chicago economist Milton Friedman in the 1970s and from some Delaware corporate takeover cases, beginning with *Smith v. van Gorkum* in 1984. That case held that in a takeover situation, the board owed a duty to stockholders to take the highest price, regardless of other considerations. I think it was wrongly decided, but it now has been the law for 35 years, so my opinion means nothing.

American corporate law in general, even in Delaware, however, is clear that corporate directors owe their duties *to the corporation as an entity*, not to its stockholders. That is hard for people to grasp because the corporation is only a conceptual entity. Can the directors—who are told by the law to manage the business and affairs of the corporation— owe their duties of care and loyalty to that same conceptual entity whose business they are supposed to manage? Yes. And in the exercise of those duties, the directors are protected from liability to anybody if they have made business judgments in good faith and with reasonable diligence and no conflict of interests. This "business judgment rule" is at the heart of Delaware corporate law.

Let's look at an example: Suppose a corporation has a decision to make between sinking more money into a part of its business that is losing money or to abandon that part of its business. And suppose it decides to sink more money. And then suppose that part of the business still loses money. And then suppose the directors eventually decide they have to abandon that part of the business after all, even though they have recently sunk more money into it.

Can a stockholder bring an action against the directors on the ground that the directors wasted the corporation's—and thereby the stockholders'—money? No. And there are three points here.

First, the stockholder does not have "standing"—that is, the right to sue—the directors, except in a representative capacity through a "derivative action" *on behalf of the corporation*. That is because the directors owe their duties only to the corporation, not to stockholders directly.

Second, if the stockholder does bring the lawsuit derivatively and wins, the stockholder can receive nothing for herself. Whatever recovery from the directors will go only into the corporation's bank account, not the stockholder's.

Third, in the derivative suit against the directors, the directors will be entitled to invoke the business judgment rule as a defense. And in order to win on behalf of the corporation, the stockholder will have to show that either

(1) the directors had a conflict of interests with the corporation, or

(2) that the directors failed to use the diligence and care that an ordinarily prudent person would use in the circumstances, or

(3) that the directors acted in bad faith.

The stockholder will not be permitted to second-guess the business judgment of the directors in the exercise of their duty to manage the corporation that the law has imposed on them, even if in hindsight that judgment turns out to have been wrong.

That the contrasting *Smith* v. *van Gorkum* rubric applies only to cases where the company is for sale was confirmed two years later in *Revlon v. MacAndrews & Forbes.*

Even critics of the existing Delaware law, such as Steven Pearlstein, agree that the stockholder-centric version of corporate law that many people think is the law is not actually the law.

Here is Pearlstein's diagnosis:

"There may be no more pernicious example of the way the ethic of "greed is good" has been woven into the fabric of modern life than the widespread embrace of the idea that companies must put shareholder interests above all others. Much of what we perceive to be wrong with American capitalism is a consequence of this misguided ideology, *which has no basis in law, history or logic.*" (p. 46) [Italics added by ML.]

Pearlstein goes on to explain how the case law has been misinterpreted (by non-lawyers) to become a broad mandate to emphasize stockholder interests rather than a mandate to manage the corporation in the best interests of the business.

Although Pearlstein agrees that that is not the law, he argues that the popular perversion of the law is so pervasive that, from a practical point of view, it might as well be the law—and therefore the law should be changed to give directors explicit obligations to stakeholders.

I do not deny that the overly-shareholder-centric idea that Pearlstein describes has general currency. But rather than make a radical change in the law, I suggest that we should not give in to the people who have perpetrated the perversion of the law. Instead, we should educate people about what the law requires and what the law permits. We should educate about the business judgment rule that protects directors who act in good faith, even if they turn out to be mistaken. And we should educate people about the long-term nature of corporate interests and how the market actually values them.

In the end, because the shareholders own the residual earnings of the corporation, they benefit from whatever the corporation earns. Thus, the proper management of the corporation, whatever it is, ends up benefitting the shareholders—but as the law suggests, that benefit is derivative, through the corporation, not direct.

It is essential for the rest of us to understand that in order to make profits, boards of directors must emphasize the interests of customers and therefore of the people who serve customers. The profit motive therefore is sufficient to make boards of directors pay attention to the core constituencies of customers and employees.

Some boards of directors do fall down on the job. That is especially true when the directors are politicians. But such corporations tend not to last very long. Think Enron or WorldCom in the early 2000s.

Productivity

On an economy-wide basis, increases in "productivity" are extremely important because they are the way that the total economic pie is increased. And as I have noted, increasing the size of the pie is the best way to increase the economic wellbeing of the middle class.

Productivity in that sense is measured as gross domestic product (GDP) divided by the number of hours that people have worked in wage-paying jobs. "Productivity" goes up when an average hour of work has produced more GDP.

But national productivity has little significance for an individual firm.

A business cares more about the profit it can earn from an hour of work than about its output. Thus, a single business has a different view of productivity than the economy does.

Increasing profits may mean educating workers better, getting better workers, making innovations that eliminate the need for some workers, making innovations that create new products or new markets, investing in machines that do workers' work more cheaply, finding new markets, outsourcing products or processes to other companies that may have lower costs, increasing quality, raising prices, or a host of other possible mechanisms.

The questions for this section of the corporate governance discussion are (1) to what extent would it be useful for boards of directors to be *legally required* to consider the impact of their decisions on the employees of the corporation? And (2) would it be beneficial for corporations to be required to have a percentage of their boards of directors be elected by employees?

Except when they have decided to sell the business, boards of directors usually do consider the impact of their actions on the employees of the business. That is only logical because workers are a key input and the quality of their work is influenced by whether employees think the board of directors cares about them.

What do companies do to win the respect of their employees? That varies greatly, of course. But in a tight labor market, companies tend to do more.

Many large American employers currently have programs designed to make it possible for employees to become better at their jobs or learn new skills that will help them to fill new jobs that new technologies are creating. But the success of these programs seems mediocre. Some companies, such as Amazon, seem to be having more success than others. My guess is that Amazon's relative success comes because it has a better idea of the skills its employees will need in the future than most companies do.

Another company that seems to do better than most is Southwest Airlines. According to libertarian economist John Cochrane,

> "Southwest Airlines' ability to turn an airplane around in 20 minutes, compared to the hour or so it took in the 1970s, and still does at many larger airlines, is just as much an increase in productivity as installing the latest gadget.

> "The key insight of modern growth theory is that, as a result of the process described above [the example was rock climbing], the larger the group studying any problem, the faster knowledge advances. If 1000 people are figuring out how to climb, and each of their good ideas disseminates through the group, each member of the group gets to use new ideas more quickly than if there are 100 people doing it."

That is a great insight: How should a company best harness all the good ideas that its employees might have and build on them? Most likely, in Southwest's case, that process was built on the ethos of employee quality that Southwest already had.

Where did the Southwest Airlines employee ethos come from? At least from stories that are told, it came from the top—and from the time of the airline's founding. The same appears to have been true of the other companies ranked highly by their employees that I discussed in Chapter 4—employee focus seems to have come from the top and to have begun early in the company's history. It appears to be quite difficult for a company that has not respected its employees to make a turnaround and win employees' affection.

Cases where companies and employees have worked together to improve employee efficiency are win-win propositions—both sides benefit.

Where the rubber meets the road, however, is when a company has to decide whether to spend money on new machines (or outsource to a less expensive jurisdiction) in order to become more efficient. New machines mean that the business will use less labor, and thus it will produce more per hour of labor. Although that investment may raise the wages of some remaining employees—for example, those who learn to run the new machines—in the ordinary situation, it will lay off a greater number of other employees. And in the outsourcing case, a few employees may benefit by taking a quality-checking role, but many others likely will be laid off.

If the board of directors had employee representatives, would they vote for spending money on the new machines or the outsourcing? Would they not try to prevent either one? Should they not try to prevent the layoff of people they represent? If employees had a right to sue the board for not paying enough attention to their perspective, would they not do that to prevent investments and policies that would put them out of work? Company level profitability and company level worker interests frequently are adverse to each other.

Productivity benefits workers in an economy generally through a long-term process, but within a particular company, the opposite often is true. If you would like details about how these processes work, Daron Acemoglu, one of MIT's great economists, and Pascual Restrepo of Boston University have recently published "Automation and New Tasks: How Technology Displaces and Reinstates Labor", Journal of Economic Perspectives— Volume 33, Number 2—Spring 2019— Pages 3–30. It is quite technical, but I think it describes reality.

Thus, it is difficult to connect firm-level data with national data. Corporate governance concerns firm-level data, whereas economic commentators are concerned with national and international data. The next section will discuss some national data because that is what tends to drive public discussion.

Have Productivity Increases Not Been Passed along to Workers in Recent Years?

If Not, Why Not?

Productivity should be the driver of progress for workers as well as for stockholders. Yet some ways of looking at the data appear to show that over the last twenty years or so, the benefits of productivity have gone more to stockholders and corporate officers than to workers. The extent of that disparity is open to debate, and the numbers are, I confess, beyond my ability to estimate reliably. But the subject is important for evaluating whether workers are getting a fair shake in today's capitalist economy. Therefore I will show you a few sets of graphs that at least should convince you that the answers to such questions are not as clear as some people say they are.

The following graph from a Barclay's Bank study shows that labor's share of GDP declined fairly precipitously from 2000 to 2007. You will note that the decline began only around 2000, not in, say, 1981, when the Reagan Administration adopted less labor-friendly policies. Whatever happened around 2000 must have been quite dramatic.

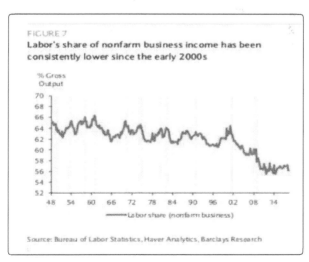

FIGURE 7

Labor's share of nonfarm business income has been consistently lower since the early 2000s

Source: Bureau of Labor Statistics, Haver Analytics, Barclays Research

I do not know what happened in 2000 to cause this decline. We do know that China came into the WTO and introduced competition from workers who were paid significantly less than American workers. And we do know as well that the foreign component of sales by U.S. companies was rising at the same time, suggesting that maybe the GDP data were growing but the U.S. labor component was not growing.

David Autor, an outstanding MIT economist, recently published a paper that outlined the reasons that he believes workers with no more than a high school diploma have fared badly in remuneration over the last several decades. David H. Autor, "Work of the Past, Work of the Future", AEA Papers and Proceedings 2019, 109: 1–32. In my opinion, David Autor is the leading analyst of this subject.

Autor's recent paper finds that, especially in urban areas, the jobs available to men without more schooling than a high school diploma have changed—for the worse. The jobs (middle skill jobs, economists call them) those workers used to occupy have disappeared, mostly because of technological changes, and those workers have had to take lower- paying jobs.

The overall picture that Autor paints at the beginning of his paper can be summarized by his first set of graphs—reproduced below.

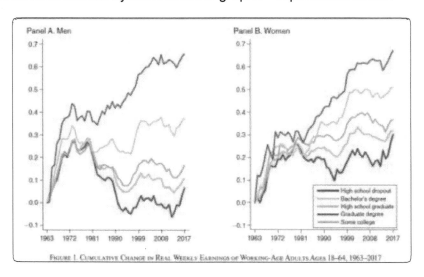

FIGURE 1. CUMULATIVE CHANGE IN REAL WEEKLY EARNINGS OF WORKING-AGE ADULTS AGES 18–64, 1963–2017

As you can see, since about 1980, weekly earnings of men with no more than a high school education have been declining, while earnings of better educated men have taken off, even while their number has grown. The picture for women has not been as bleak on a comparative basis, but women's earnings began from a lower, discrimination-induced base. Autor points out that the decline in the earnings of lower-educated men is not peculiarly American; it has been occurring in many economically advanced nations. And if you were working in an office around 1980, as I was, you would have seen how the first wave of computers affected almost all middle skill jobs.

Autor also shows that this process has had three phases:

> "The progression of inequality over these five and a half decades can be roughly divided into three epochs: (i) the ten-year interval between 1963 and 1972, when real wages rose robustly and evenly among all education and gender groups; (ii) the interregnum between 1973 and 1979 when, following the first US oil shock [and the accompanying inflation], real earnings growth stagnated throughout the distribution; and (iii) the era of secularly rising wage inequality from 1980 forward, where wages rose robustly among the most-educated and fell in real terms among the least-educated—most strikingly, among men with less than a bachelor's degree."

Thus, Autor finds that changes in the nature of work, rather than changes in policies or any number of other possible causes, was the principal cause of the decline. If he is correct, then the explanation that the decline was caused by the decline in labor union representation is not correct, and that has implications for the kind of policy we need that could promote better earnings for this class of workers.

David Autor, this time with several collaborators, have an even newer paper that sheds more light on this subject. The new paper, to be published in the December 2019 issue of the Quarterly Journal of Economics, shows that the biggest changes in the labor share of the fruits of production has been between firms, rather than within firms. That is, over the last few decades, "superstar" firms have gained productivity much more rapidly than more ordinary firms. This is due to numerous factors, but they include better investment in productivity improvement, more patent protection, and significant economies of scale. These superstar firms pay better, but they employ more educated workers. That pattern holds true in substantially all economically advanced nations, Autor and his collaborators find. Thus it is unlikely that U.S.-centric forces are principally the cause. David Autor, David Dorn, Lawrence F. Katz, Christina Patterson, and John Van Reenen "The Fall of the Labor Share and the Rise of Superstar Firms", December 2019, Quarterly Journal of Economics, Forthcoming.

That the rise of superstar firms and changes in the nature of work are the principal causes of the decline in the labor share makes sense to me. And they are not causes that changes in public policy probably should seek to reverse. Those causes being the principal ones does not, however rule out less benign causes being at work as well. One of those that Autor and his co-authors explicitly leave open for further research is the degree to which superstar firms, after achieving their status, are able to use lobbying and similar methods to prevent inroads on their status due to competition. So much depends on government policies that it is possible that superstar effects are exaggerated and sustained by capture of the legislative and regulatory mechanisms. Whether further research will demonstrate that to be true remains to be seen.

Which way of looking at the earnings/productivity issue is right? I give great credibility to the work of David Autor and of Daron Acemoglu, who are at the top of their profession and are not driven by a particular ideology.

Regardless of the causes, however, I am convinced that the meager earnings of less educated Americans is a problem that has to be addressed. It is not going to go away.

But the means by which the problem is addressed matter a lot. In designing the means, policy makers should be aware that the companies that employ the largest numbers of American workers tend to be the companies that have made the least progress in productivity and that tend to have the smallest profit margins. The aggregate data on the division of productivity increases tends to obscure these facts because the more successful modern technology companies account for fewer employees but a large proportion of productivity improvement. Thus, a part of the post-1999 statistical disparity is explained by the success of technology companies.

By contrast with the technology companies, a major grocer like Kroger, for example, employs many people at modest wages, has low profit margins, has made relatively little productivity progress, and has returned relatively meager results to its stockholders. (I do not have comparable data on Trader Joe's, Wegman's and H.E.B., all of which also are grocers, because as private companies they do not report their results.)

Apple, as a representative of the tech class of companies, has relatively few—but better paid—employees, has made great strides in productivity, has high profit margins, and has made large returns for its stockholders. Apple invests significantly in its future technology, but it also buys back its stock because its cashflow is so strong. Tyler Cowen, an outstanding economist at George Mason University, contends that, "The real increase in inequality has come from the gap between the very strong super firms and firms which are more mediocre performers." And that view tends to be confirmed by David Autor's most recent work.

Amazon, to round out the major style possibilities, is an outlier statistically because it has become a major employer and invests successfully in productivity improvements, but its profit margins in its core business are small and its profitability is not strong, yet the stock market loves it and accords it a high valuation relative to its earnings. Is Amazon a new paradigm case—or is it just an outlier? My guess is that Amazon is just an outlier but that its success as an investment is an indication that the stock market in fact rewards long-term thinking.

The top tech companies continue to be long-term thinkers and the market continues to reward them for it. They invest both in physical infrastructure, such as buildings and undersea cables, and research and development. The top tech companies are the biggest long-term investors, but, contrary to common belief, American corporate spending on research and development and capital improvements, by all companies combined, are at all-time highs. There are companies that do not invest in the future, but they are not the most successful ones.

Moral Capitalism

"Moral capitalism" is a phrase associated with a set of principles promulgated in 1994 by a group of international executives called the Caux Roundtable. (Caux is a town in Switzerland where the group first met.) The Caux principles are spelled out and discussed in a book called *Moral Capitalism* by Stephen Young that was published in 2003.

Basically, moral capitalism asks boards of directors and managements to manage each business with due regard for all its various *stakeholders*, such as customers, employees, equity owners, lenders, suppliers, and the broader community. It does not ask that obligations to these stakeholders be enshrined in law, but asks that they be paid attention to in the management process. As such, moral capitalism is addressed to each company's inner soul.

It is easy to dismiss that sort of hortatory standards as unrealistic or as promoting weak managements that will be taken advantage of by more self-centered ones. But I find a great deal to like about the moral capitalism concept.

"Moral capitalism presumes that all—rich and poor alike—possess a moral sense." *Moral Capitalism* at p. 65. Thus moral capitalism places itself in a universalist religious tradition that I think harks back to the moral deism of America's founders. ("We hold these truths to be self evident . . .")

Moral capitalism describes corporate governance as a "stewardship", which I find a useful way of looking at it. And the Caux principles call for "character" in corporate decision-making, not merely compliance with laws and regulations.

Indeed, similar to my description of capitalism and democracy earlier in this book, *Moral Capitalism* says (p.99) that:

> "Neither moral capitalism nor democracy contemplates final outcomes for people because they are only procedures for the expression of personal power . . . [B]oth rest on the same fundamental principle of respect for human autonomy and dignity. Moral capitalism and democracy are both process systems, where procedure and playing by the rules is elevated over substantive goals and objectives."

And at p. 100, *Moral Capitalism* says, "The markets are an open process respectful of pluralism." Later on, the book explains further:

> "Consumers provide the compass for capitalism, employees do the work, owners make the arrangements, and suppliers feed the machinery of business, but competition hones business decision making, always driving our attention towards the needs of others." (p. 151)

> "All that is required for the [moral capitalism] ideal to happen is the exercise of self-restraint, the demonstration of moral character, on the part of business decision makers." (p. 153)

I wish I could be more optimistic about a great many business decision makers actually doing that. My experience over many years is that, although some business decision makers have a moral character that they can bring to bear, in too many cases, they do not do so. Thus petty bribery, over-reaching and other immoral practices are rife in the business world—as they are almost everywhere. It is not only businesses that lack good moral compasses.

If we put the Caux principles together with a disclosure system, perhaps there is a way to make moral capitalism more workable on a broader scale than just those few companies that are willing to embrace the principles. If all sizable companies were required to enunciate a set of principles, covering specific areas of operations and relationships, then be required to evaluate their own compliance with those principles on an annual basis, then maybe, over a period of years, some progress could be made without imposing new conduct-oriented legal obligations.

University of Chicago Professor (and former Governor of the Central Bank of India) Raghuram Rajan seems to agree that this might be a useful idea. He wrote for Bloomberg on May 1, 2019:

"Given the considerable leeway corporate boards already have, it would be a step in the right direction for them to specify whose interests, including workers', they are protecting. That would allow investors to better gauge the trade-offs a board will make. It would also give core stakeholders greater confidence to invest in the corporation.

Most important in these populist times, corporate boards can also then avoid unnecessary political flak by identifying their core stakeholders—those who make financial or other long-term real investments in the firm. That would not just circumvent progressive critics, it would also be the right thing to do."

For sure, consultants would love my suggested disclosure and self-evaluation system. They would see a lucrative business both in designing loophole-ridden principles and in annually whitewashing half-hearted compliance. Every new requirement makes some set of lawyers, accountants and consultants happy. But beyond token compliance, I think it possible that progress gradually could be made. As I said earlier, most companies that have a pro-customer or pro-worker ethos adopted it early, when it was a founder's tenet. But forced to review the subject later on, a management could see that some very successful companies have it and might be persuaded to move in that direction rather than having to defend another business emphasis.

The difficulty of defining moral capitalism in a way that is practical is illustrated by a June 24, 2019 op-ed by a Georgetown University history professor Michael Kazin. He elegantly traced the history of the Democratic Party and pointed out that a moral capitalism could be key to pulling the current strands together. But he did not suggest how to implement a moral capitalism.

Professor Kazin's lack of a published implementation strategy does not mean that we should abandon the goal of a more moral capitalism. But it should inoculate us against simplistic answers.

The "B" Corp and "Benefit Corporation" Concepts

Some commentators think there is a need for a type of for-profit corporation that can voluntarily adopt legal standards that recognize the several corporate constituencies, including employees, customers, the community and the environment, as well as specifically adopting a long-term view. For this purpose, several states have enabled the creation of "Benefit" corporations that must adhere to such standards, and the Model Business Corporation Act promulgated by the American Law Institute includes provision for Benefit corporations. To date, few corporations have converted to Benefit corporation status, but a fair number of startups have adopted it.

A "B' corp, another recent new name, is an ordinary for-profit corporation that has been certified by an international entity called B Lab as complying with high standards of transparency, attention to constituencies, and the environment. Many companies (though most of them are not large) have been so certified, and although certification does not impose any legal requirements, if does impose an obligation to engage in an annual independent assessment program.

One can look at the "B corp" designation as a sort of experiment as to how a suggestion like a disclosure and self-assessment program might work. Voluntary compliance by application and designation can give signals to sensitive potential customers that this is an entity that they should want to deal with, but that is not likely to make the kind of major impact that a mandatory self-assessment system might make.

Has the Business Roundtable Changed American Corporate Governance?

On August 19, 2019, the Business Roundtable (BRT), an important group of about 200 large American and Canadian companies, issued a new statement of governance principles that embraced the stakeholder idea. The BRT, which previously had made shareholder primacy the centerpiece of its governance philosophy, declared that the purpose of a corporation is to promote "An Economy That Serves All Americans". The new corporate mantra is long-term value for shareholders while serving other stakeholders as well. The core of the statement is:

"We commit to:

> Delivering value to our customers. We will further the tradition of American companies leading the way in meeting or exceeding customer expectations.
> Investing in our employees. This starts with compensating them fairly and providing important benefits. It also includes supporting them through training and education that help develop new skills for a rapidly changing world. We foster diversity and inclusion, dignity and respect.
> Dealing fairly and ethically with our suppliers. We are dedicated to serving as good partners to the other companies, large and small, that help us meet our missions.
> Supporting the communities in which we work. We respect the people in our communities and protect the environment by embracing sustainable practices across our businesses.
> Generating long-term value for shareholders, who provide the capital that allows companies to invest, grow and innovate. We are committed to transparency and effective engagement with shareholders.

Each of our stakeholders is essential. We commit to deliver value to all of them, for the future success of our companies, our communities and our country."

A statement of principles that promises so much can mean different things to different people. But for sure it is very changed in tone from what one might call the corporate triumphalism that pre-dated the Great Recession. It is a statement that corporations have obligations to others besides shareholders. And it reflects the ethos of the Caux Principles and the concept of Moral Capitalism.

Both the right and the left have expressed reservations—or even dismay—at the new BRT principles. On the left, the lack of any enforcement mechanism has led to denigration that the real purpose of the new principles is lip service to prevent anything like Senator Warren's Accountable Capitalism Act from becoming law. On the right, there is a fear that the new principles are leading American companies away from profit making and toward whatever do-good policies management might want to adopt.

Both these charges make sense. The BRT statement is a compromise. But I think it is a good compromise because it will encourage American companies to continue policies that will benefit their businesses in the long run, while retaining flexibility to pursue profitability as their primary goal. As I said at the beginning of this chapter, most large companies have considered various stakeholders for a long time. The BRT statement validates that.

The one major stakeholder that the BRT statement includes that few companies have emphasized in the past is the environment. That new inclusion has horrified some on the right. But realistically, consumers are becoming more aware that companies whose goods and services they buy have an impact on the environment in ways that they—the consumers—care about. That consumer awareness is driving companies to demonstrate environmental responsibility—and they would do so even had the BRT not spoken.

Sweden's Unique Bargaining System

A number of the suggested corporate governance changes are based on European systems. Those systems include, prominently, the Swedish system and the German system, each of which I will discuss briefly.

Sweden also is important because when one asks Americans who say they prefer socialism to capitalism what country has the socialism they would like America to have, many of them name Sweden. Sweden does have some unique and attractive attributes, but it is not a socialist country. Indeed, Sweden has, over the last 20 years, become among the most capitalist countries in the world.

Sweden does have a national system of bargaining between representatives of management and representatives of labor that is attractive and unusual. The representatives represent not merely individual companies, but entire industries. Thus Sweden acts, in effect, as a single organism in setting wages, and domestic competitors cannot gain an advantage over each other by paying less to their employees.

The result is a fairly flat pay system, where those at the top make not that much more than those at the bottom. And because those at the bottom make more, companies have incentives to use capital/machines to reduce the number of employees and thereby to become more efficient. The result is attractive. (Currently, the system seems to be under attack due to recent emigration into Sweden, but I will put that to one side as possibly a temporary problem.)

Sweden has combined its unique pay determination system with a relatively free market approach to business. It is not socialist in its approach to business, although its safety net is better than most. And Sweden tends to be ranked quite high in international competitiveness ratings, for whatever reason.

Sweden's is indeed a remarkable system, and one that many Americans might like to emulate. But Americans should be realistic about Sweden. Sweden's system grows out of a shared history and tradition. Sweden has fewer people than metropolitan NYC and its population is fairly homogeneous, both in background and in education. By contrast, the vast melting pot that is the United States has nowhere near these attributes of homogeneity, ease of communication, trust, or history. In a sense, Sweden acts as a single organism. That would not be possible in nation as riven as the U.S., with its diverse economy, history of individualism, and diversity of peoples.

Thus, although I appreciate the appeal of the Swedish system to many Americans, I would urge that Sweden's form of managed capitalism, even though it is not socialism, is not a model on which the U.S. could build successfully.

The German Co-Determination Example

Senator Warren's proposed Accountable Capitalism Act is based loosely on the German system of co-determination, in which worker representatives are allocated between a third and half of the seats on each large company's "supervisory board". This gives workers a say in the supervisory board's key functions of selecting management, setting management's compensation, and making overall corporate strategy. Under the German system, stockholders elect whatever part of the supervisory board is not allocated to labor, the supervisory board elects the "management board", and the management board runs the company day-to-day. Even when labor elects half of the supervisory board, however, it does not have 50% control of the board's decision-making because the chairman has two votes and the stockholder representatives on the board elect the chairman.

Many German companies also have works councils in which labor has an input in how factories and other workplaces are run.

This system of management-labor cooperation began in about 1850, more than 150 years ago, when, after the failed socialist Revolution of 1848, the German government gave labor a little power in order to avoid another socialist revolution. German labor's involvement in management continued to grow, both after WWI and after WWII, as German governments and U.S. authorities sought to dampen Germans' continuing attraction to socialism. Thus, while co-determination and its supportive structure are not themselves socialism, they were designed to appear to provide workers with the same type of benefits as socialism.

This seemed to suit both German managers and workers, especially in businesses that were largely technical in nature. The ethos is described by the word *technik*, which underscores the importance of technical expertise and the traditional German strength in precision manufacturing. Highly skilled workers and engineers have been respected in the German system more than in traditional American manufacturing, which has relied more on the assembly line than on the machine shop.

Co-determination also has tended to make environmental protection a more important element of German corporate policies than American ones. This makes the German system attractive to younger Americans, who appear to be more concerned about the environment than older Americans.

The German system gives less power to workers, however, than its formal structure might appear to provide. That is because the stockholdings of major German companies were, until quite recently, highly concentrated in the hands of major banks, insurance companies and money managers. Thus, the typical German company was an oligarchy, and it supported the dual board/co-determination system without much interference from the market.

That system is under attack, however, as shareholdings have become diversified and institutional holders have become more subject to market forces,

By 2018, German institutions were no longer the largest shareholders, as U.S.-based index fund managers had taken over the top places. As with most large U.S. corporations, the companies in the German DAX 30 have Vanguard and Black Rock, through the index funds they manage, almost always as passive shareholders, as their largest owners. Thus the oligarchic coziness of the German ownership pattern has been ameliorated. But the shareholder orientation of the supervisory board has not.

The German law is different from Senator Warren's proposal in many ways. One that I think important is that, like current American law, under German law, only the company can sue members of the supervisory board for breach of their obligations, and a lawsuit can be brought by shareholders only in an action similar to an American derivative action such as I described above. Thus, although the supervisory board is required to give attention to the needs of various stakeholders, only shareholders are entitled to enforce their rights in court.

An interesting (and maybe quite telling) thing to wonder about is the relative stock market value accorded to German companies compared with American companies. The value of stock markets as a percent of GDP may not be the best measure of relative value, but probably it has some validity. The following graph from the Federal Reserve Bank of St. Louis compares the German and American stock market values since 1975. (The American stock market, as represented by the S&P 500, is the top line. The lower line is the German stock market, as represented by the DAX 30.)

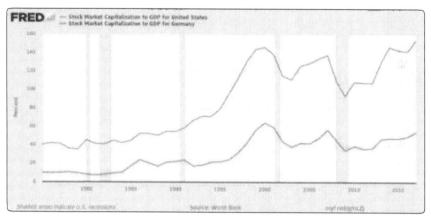

As you can see, the American stock market is consistently higher as a percentage of GDP than the German stock market.

To similar effect, in 2019, the price/earnings ratio (p.e.) for German stocks is about 13, while it is about 20 for American stocks. Again, this is not an exact comparison because the nature of the companies in the respective indexes is not the same. But the data suggest that there may be something about German companies that makes their earnings not as highly valued by the market as American companies' earnings.

One study (in 2000) found a 26% stock market discount due to equal board representation by labor in German firms.

Over the 30 years May 1989 to May 2019 (the DAX index benchmark began in 1988), the S&P 500 with dividends reinvested grew 788% compared with the DAX (including dividends) that grew 729% (based on data from Yahoo Finance). The two indices are quite different in that the DAX includes only 30 of Germany's largest companies and the sector makeup is different, reflecting the industrial differences between the two nations, but each index represents a fair picture of its nation's stock market performance. Thus, it appears, at least over the 30-year period that we can measure, the returns have been roughly comparable.

Thus, although the DAX has consistently accorded a lower p.e. to German companies than the S&P 500 has accorded to American companies, the consistency of the difference has allowed that over the 30-year period, returns have been similar.

To what extent the differences in p.e values may be influenced by the difference in corporate governance systems I do not know. But if making the U.S. system like the German system resulted in any significant diminution in the price to earnings multiples of American companies, the resulting decline in market prices would be devastating to American pension funds (already underfunded in many cases), as well as to individual stockholders and, through them, to aggregate consumer demand. That might not be a risk that the nation should want to run, even though the 30-year return data suggest that the losses might be a one-time event.

My bottom line is that although the dual board/co-determination idea has appeal, its potential dangers far outweigh its potential benefits. And co-determination without the dual board (like the Warren proposal) would not have the weight of fairly successful experience behind it.

Moreover, there are signs in Germany that the public does not regard the German corporate system as "socially just" or as providing enough support for workers who lose jobs due to globalization or technological change. Populism is on the rise in Germany, too.

The Mutual Form of Ownership

There are other forms of ownership, of course, besides the usual for-profit corporation.

MassMutual (formerly Massachusetts Mutual Life Insurance Company) began business in 1851 and today serves something like 5 million customers. One of their ads recently reminded me about the potential advantages of the mutual form ownership. It promotes the "mutual life" in which people help each other "mutually". The ads are powerful—and a powerful reminder that there are American businesses that are established not so much for profit as to benefit their customers. In most mutual formats, the customers own the business entity and receive dividends representing some of the profits. In practice, however, mutual institutions are run by self-perpetuating boards of directors or trustees. Formal ownership has very little say. As such, mutuals are useful at the sufferance of the elites that run them. But MassMutual has been in business in that form for a very long time, with a continuing theme of mutual benefit, as have a number of other life insurance companies.

Life insurance is one American business where companies have been successful in mutual form. Savings banks and savings and loan associations were another for quite a long time, and credit unions are a type that has relatively flourished in recent years.

The mutual form originated in Scotland in the early 19th century, with the first American mutual (a savings bank) being established in New York in 1819. I knew the New York mutual savings banks quite well, having represented the Savings Banks Association of New York State from about 1968 to 1984. When I began that representation, there were 120 savings banks in New York, all of which were in mutual form and most of which had been founded in the 19th century. By 1984, some of them had failed and many of them had converted to stock form. Many more converted to stock form over the next ten years. Today there are very few mutuals left in New York State. Mergers also played a role in their dwindling number.

The catalyst for the failures, mergers and conversions was the mismatch between the maturity of the assets of the savings banks and the maturity of their liabilities. The liabilities substantially all were due on demand. But the assets were long-term and at fixed rates. Therefore, when inflation (and therefore interest rates) took off in the 1970s, the savings banks were left having to pay high market rates for their deposits while their long-term assets stayed at the lower historical rates. Thus they either hemorrhaged money (if they did not pay the high current rates on deposits) or suffered negative earnings (if they did pay the high rates on their deposits). Either one was a recipe for insolvency and failure. And several of them failed in the early 1980s as result.

The same thing happened to savings and loan associations, a majority of which also were organized in mutual form. That led to the savings and loan debacle and the insolvency of the savings and loan associations' federal insurer—a process that took until 1989 to resolve. My book *High Rollers* is a history of that financial era.

Those failures brought opprobrium on the mutual form of ownership. But in truth, the mutual form of ownership did not cause the problem. The problem was caused by federal polices that had effectively mandated that savings institutions put themselves in the untenable position of borrowing short and lending long. That was what caused the havoc.

In the 1970s and early 1980s, not only did the long-short problem slay the mutuals, but the competitive landscape changed as well. Some of the new competition came from the Federal Government itself in the form of Fannie Mae and Freddie Mac that had lower funding costs and, without branch systems, lower operating costs. But part of the competition came from government shackles being released that permitted new competitors such as money market mutual funds and small denomination Treasury bonds.

What government regulation had maintained as a fairly cozy club in which mutual institutions competed almost exclusively with each other became open competition. See my 2017 book *Instability* for details of how repressive regulation kept the lid on competition in the 1950s and 1960s—until the steam generated by inflation blew the lid off the pressure cooker of financial repression in the late 1970s.

I was there and witnessed the changes firsthand. As an example of cultural change, in the 1960s and most of the 1970s, the cozy New York mutual savings bank industry had a summer meeting of industry leaders. It was two days of morning meetings and golfing afternoons somewhere nice in upstate New York. (The Otesaga Hotel in Cooperstown, the Gideon Putnam Hotel in Saratoga Springs, and the Pine Tree Point Club on the St. Lawrence River were prominent venues.) A feature of these get-togethers was an after dinner singalong (mostly old songs) with a banker at the piano. I confess that I participated lustily. But by the late 1970s, there were no more singalongs. The business had become quite serious. Participants were wondering how their institutions could survive, and the meetings were focused on that. Frivolity was out.

Were the savings banks of the 1960s and 1970s efficient intermediaries, as some commentators (such as Steven Pearlstein) have suggested? I think many of them were not. They flourished only because regulation of interest rates on deposits allowed them to compete more or less successfully. Without that form of governmental financial repression, I do not think they could have had a big enough spread between what they paid for deposits and what they earned on mortgages to cover the costs of their expensive branch systems.

In the 21st century, however, the credit union industry—also organized in mutual form—appears to be thriving fairly well. In a sense, a credit union is a co-op. And I see no reason that the co-op form of ownership should not be permitted for any kind of business and be permitted to compete with the standard business corporation model. Based on history, however, I would not predict that co-ops will take over large segments of the business world.

What Makes Companies Profitable?

Companies become profitable not by thinking about stockholders (stockholders neither buy nor make nor sell products or services) but by thinking about customers (number one) and about the people who create and sell the products and services that the customers buy (number two). In the real world, number three has to be thinking about how to prevent competition, such as by using patents, designs and trademarks or otherwise erecting what Warren Buffett calls "moats". These are the imperatives of business. And profitable companies today, just as much as 40 or 50 years ago, have these priorities. Amazon, remarkably, seems to stay one jump ahead of the competition by being technologically more innovative in ways to serve customers and Apple continues to figure out ways to make its products consumer must-haves.

Not only are Apple and Amazon stock market darlings, but my research shows that companies that think long-term and are customer oriented are rewarded by higher market multiples. And long-term investing increasingly is what the wealthiest individuals are looking for.

The impression that customer orientation and other sound business practices are disrespected arises principally from "financial engineering" by means of which some companies seek to maximize their stock prices without increasing their long-term value. Often egged on by dissident stockholders, corporations lever up (borrow) in order to buy back stock and increase its price. That short-term benefit makes the corporation more fragile over the long term. Other similar practices have similar effects.

My research suggests that the market does not reward high financial leverage over the long term. But it frequently is rewarded in the short term. It makes a company's stock price more volatile, and sometimes that suits the interests of management. See Justin Fox, *The Myth of the Rational Market* at p. 280 for more explanation.

Such short-term thinking not only is not required of boards of directors; it even can be argued that the law discourages such strategies. But the realities of corporate life frequently seem to require giving in to the pressures of dissident stockholders.

Was even Apple a victim of that kind of pressure from Carl Icahn when it borrowed and used a large part of the borrowing to buy back stock in recent years? Or was Icahn simply correct that Apple's cash stockpile was too large but was kept offshore for tax reasons and therefore could be used effectively only by borrowing against it? In this case, I come down on Icahn's side because Apple's leverage remains modest, because its borrowing rates were low, and because it continues to invest in research and development at a high rate. Thus the Apple case shows that knee-jerk reactions to "financial engineering" may not always be correct.

Justin Fox argues that integrity is a material factor in a company's long- term success. And I agree. At p. 285 of *The Myth of the Rational Market*, Fox quotes an economist's PowerPoint slide as summarizing what corporate integrity means:

➤ "Keep your commitments and promises on time or

➤ When you have failed to keep a commitment or promise, you:

    ○ Acknowledge that failure as soon as you realize it,

    ○ And clean up any mess you created for those who were counting on your commitment and promises."

Good stuff, I think.

CHAPTER 7

The Crucial Role of Antitrust Laws

A defense of capitalism must acknowledge that competition needs to be protected from the natural tendency of businesses to seek monopoly power. Adam Smith knew that back in 1776. And Congress recognized it long ago, in 1890, with enactment of our first antitrust law, the Sherman Act.

For over a century, the U.S. antitrust laws have two fundamental parts: anti-monopoly law in the Sherman Act of 1890, and law that prevents mergers and acquisitions from creating monopolies in the Clayton Act, last amended in 1950. Over the years, relatively few cases have been brought under the Sherman Act's anti-monopoly provisions, and since WWII, only one (AT&T, on which more below) was successful. (The Sherman Act also outlawed price fixing and some other anticompetitive practices.)

I would not go this far, but Jonathan Tepper asserts in his book *The Myth of Capitalism* that:

> "The damage to the economy [from lax antitrust enforcement] is far worse than you could imagine. The evidence is overwhelming that higher economic concentration has created a toxic cocktail of higher prices, less economic dynamism, fewer startups, lower productivity, lower wages, greater economic inequality, and damage to smaller communities. Competition has not so much declined as thudded into the abyss." (p. 37).

Tepper relates lax antitrust enforcement to the growth in inequality. He points out that antitrust enforcement was most vigorous in the period 1941 to 1980 and that that coincided with a period of relative equality. (p. 22) I think the correlation probably is coincidental because of the changes in the nature of work and international competition that I have already discussed, but there might be some causal relationship.

Regardless of its possible impact on inequality, there has been a relative paucity of antitrust enforcement in recent years. Kevin Wilson, an antitrust hawk, has used the following graph to illustrate this phenomenon:

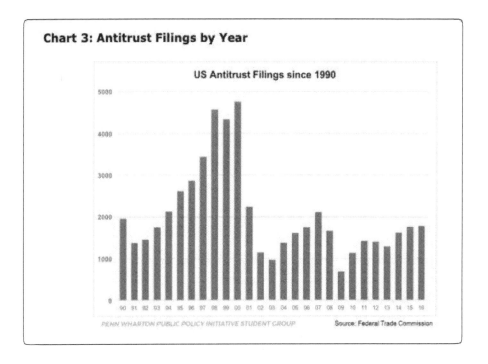

Chart 3: Antitrust Filings by Year

US Antitrust Filings since 1990

PENN WHARTON PUBLIC POLICY INITIATIVE STUDENT GROUP   Source: Federal Trade Commission

Monopolies

Senator Elizabeth Warren and many others have made it a political goal to break up the leading tech companies, such as Amazon, Facebook and Google. She sees them as dangerous monopolies. Amazon's reach is enormous. And its principal owner Jeff Bezos also owns the Washington Post, so he has a megaphone, as well.

Other theorists hark back to Justice Brandeis, who a century ago favored breaking up large business combinations on the ground that they had too much political power.

These two modern thrusts, whether they are useful or not, should be taken seriously because of the central place that competition holds in the capitalist system.

As part of any review of these ideas, however, one should recognize how much the world of commerce has been changed by the Internet and its capacity to reach so many people. The ubiquity of the Internet and its ability to create huge enterprises has important implications for antitrust law. What they are is the question.

This graph from Wikipedia illustrates the reach of the Internet:

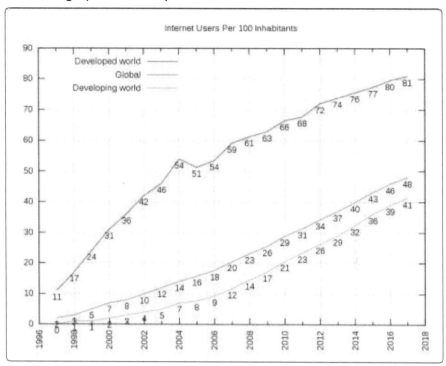

Internet Users Per 100 Inhabitants

Traditional antitrust law focused on protecting competitive markets. Much of the newer antitrust theory (by newer, I mean post-1980), as applied by the courts, has focused on actual pricing as an indication of whether competition has been curtailed. That trend seems to me a perversion (although I studied antitrust law with Robert Bork, the progenitor of the theory). Market power, as indicated by theory, is a much better guide to the future, even though it necessarily involves courts in trying to foresee future impacts—admittedly a task at which courts are not well suited. (Economists also are not so good at predicting the future, I might add—though I do not know who *is* good at it. I guess that is why we call it the future.)

Attempts to reduce antitrust questions to formulae have not been successful. I think Bork became so enamored of free market thinking that antitrust law seemed to him like an impediment to rather than a useful part of the free market capitalism he championed. His theorizing therefore pulled the teeth from enforcement.

Measuring market power in an Internet-dominated world is not so easy. And one also should bear in mind that in today's dynamic business world, leading companies come and go quite quickly. Just look at the S&P 500 (the index of America's leading companies), where over the last 20 years, those 500 leading companies have turned over almost 50%. In such a changeable world, what kind of market power is likely to be sufficiently enduring to be worth curtailing?

Lina Khan is one of the leading theorists of the 21st century revival of the Brandeis school of antitrust thinking that seeks to deal with the problems that the Internet companies pose.

I find her analysis fundamentally in step with traditional antitrust theory and the competitive markets view of capitalism. According to the New York Times, her fundamental point of view is that "The long-term interests of consumers include product quality, variety and innovation—factors best promoted through both a robust competitive process and open markets."

I agree. The question is what policies will best promote those virtues.

As reported by Rana Faroohar of the FT, Khan also says that reforms should be "platform specific". That would require that a judge or panel of wise persons (not the people as expressed through the market) decide what the structure of an entire industry should be like—on a case-by-case basis.

That is basically what courts have to do in monopoly cases. Therefore, let's briefly review the monopoly cases since WWII to see how they have turned out.

One such case was U.S. against AT&T that broke up the telephone monopoly in 1984. Breaking up the monopoly seemed like a good idea. It would lead to more competition—and it did. But technology also broke up even the smaller monopolies that the decision created. And now, just 35 years later, the communications industry looks totally different from what anyone might have imagined in 1984. And it is dominated by two of the "baby bells" that the breakup created and one subsidiary of the German equivalent. The greatest threat to their oligopoly, ironically, is Google, which is a newcomer to that field. Should Google (itself an alleged monopolist in the field of Internet search) be permitted to enlarge *its* power by competing with the three oligopolists? Where's the harm? One might argue. Only a very large company can compete in cell phone service, anyway, so adding a competitor is good. Under T-Mobile's settlement with the Department of Justice, Dish also may be able to become a competitor, too. But is Google/ Alphabet too big already?

The IBM case also is illustrative. The U.S. sued IBM in 1969, alleging that IBM had monopolized and was attempting to monopolize the "general purpose electronic digital computer system market, specifically computers designed primarily for business", in violation of the Sherman Act. The case went to trial in 1975 and finally was dismissed in 1982. In the intervening years, technological change and competition eroded IBM's monopoly position so completely that by the 1990s, IBM was reinventing itself as primarily a service business. In 1985, shortly after the case was dismissed, IBM had 405,000 employees. But by 1995, it was down to 225,000, had suffered through unprofitable years, and no one thought IBM had a monopoly on anything significant. IBM is still struggling to find a profitable niche.

It is worth noting that many others of the great companies of the 1960s, such as Eastman Kodak, Xerox, General Electric and General Motors eventually have been laid low by a combination of technological change and a failure to keep up with the competition. Market domination in the U.S. has lacked permanence.

The U.S. and 19 states sued Microsoft in 1999, principally alleging that Microsoft was using its monopoly power of the Windows operating system to prevent Netscape's browser from competing with Microsoft's browser. The case was eventually settled. Netscape faded nevertheless, due to others having better technology. The browser no longer seems such a key competitive aspect, and Windows has competitors as well, including Apple's operating system and Google's operating system, which are dominant in mobile computing. Moreover, the personal computer is close to a dinosaur, having been overtaken by the tablet and the smart phone. Microsoft is still doing very well, but Windows is no longer a monopoly product.

It was easy to break up the Standard Oil trust in 1911. There were properties—oil wells, refineries, supply lines and distribution systems—all discrete units that could be combined or not. That is not true of modern Internet-based behemoths. Something like 33 companies resulted from the Standard Oil breakup, and, perhaps ironically, they had an aggregate market value greater than that of the trust from which they were created. The same might have been true if the aluminum giant Alcoa had it lost its monopoly case in 1945. It did not. But nevertheless, today Alcoa, even after a major business reorganization, is struggling to be profitable in a globally competitive aluminum business.

Google and Amazon are the two great disrupters of the world of 2019. They are horning in on many businesses by using their technological expertise, forward business thinking, and financial wherewithal to target potentially entrenched businesses. In the same vein, Amazon, Apple and Disney are taking on Netflix in creating and streaming content. In the smart-home assistant market, Amazon is dominant at the moment, with a 70% market share, but Google and Apple are its leading competitors, with 24% and 6%, respectively.

Should the behemoths be prohibited from competing with each other? Without that, might some markets not be far less competitive?

And some markets are in such flux that it is hard to know what they will look like in a few years. What used to be known as television is a case in point, as several technologies and types of content vie for the public's favor. Amazon, Google, Disney, Comcast, Apple, Facebook, Roku, Netflix, CBS, NBC, AT&T, SONY, the sports leagues, and many smaller players vie for space and time in that world.

The smart phone wreaked havoc on MP3 players, portable GPS systems and digital cameras, as they incorporated the others' functions into a single platform. But now smart phone sales are reaching a plateau, as sales growth has stalled, according to Jake Swearingen, writing in Intelligencer:

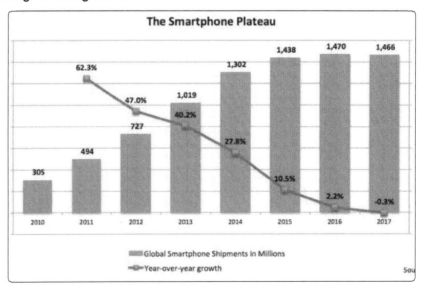

Will something replace the smart phone?

No one knows what will happen when connection to almost everything is via the much faster 5G and numerous home devices are connected and controlled through a smart phone or similar device.

And Facebook, itself only fifteen years old, already may be in decline, especially among the young. It appears that Facebook had 15 million fewer users in the U.S. in 2019 than it had in 2017, and that those still using it are using it less. According to a study by Edison Research,

> "Those age 13-34 say they are using Facebook less because they enjoy other social media sites more, their friends don't post much on Facebook, and because they are trying to avoid parents and relatives on the site."

Some analysts already are referring to Google's search business as a "legacy" business and are looking to Alphabet's other ventures for future sources of growth.

I am not suggesting that monopolies should be ignored. They are an enemy of capitalism. In *The Myth of Capitalism*, author Jonathan Tepper says:

> "Capitalism has been the greatest system in history to lift people out of poverty and create wealth, but the "capitalism" we see today in the United States is a far cry from competitive markets." Kindle location 523.

Tepper is an antitrust hawk—perhaps a bit extreme in some ways—but I agree with his basic proposition. And ideally, I suggest that the rules should be principled, not invented for particular cases and applied by clever social engineers. I also suggest that technology moves faster than the courts to defeat today's near monopolies. It is a tribute to capitalism that the rate of change in so many areas has been so great. Change may make people uncomfortable in some ways, but it also can represent progress.

All that having been said, there are some relative monopolies that may require closer regulation. Amazon's relative dominance of the platform through which online sales occur, for example, does give it a kind of market power that bears scrutiny, as Lina Khan suggests in her landmark Yale Law Journal "note", "Amazon's Antitrust Paradox". Governmental action to prevent Amazon from using the power of the platform to favor its own offerings and to impede competition may well be necessary.

Regulation also may be necessary to prevent Google, which also owns YouTube, from using its market power through control of global search to favor its own related products and services over those of its competitors. That is a classic problem that the European regulators have understood better than their American counterparts. Perhaps one of Google's practices that will be prosecuted is effectively forcing advertisers to use its services in order to place ads on YouTube.

But, curiously, Amazon's most profitable product has little to do with its dominant e-tail platform. It is the almost unrelated "cloud computing", where it competes straight-up in a market that is dominated by four very large companies: Amazon, Microsoft, Alibaba and Google. Here is a picture of that competition from the ParkMyCloud.com website:

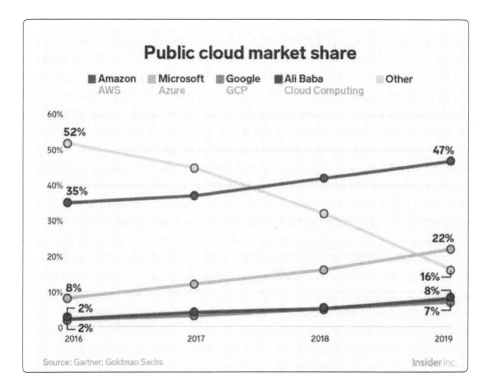

As you can see, the four big players have been taking market share at the expense of smaller players in that market. But Google and Alibaba have a long way to go to achieve high market share—and they have incentives and the financial muscle to do so.

Therefore I have to return to Lina Khan's statement about platform-specific remedies, and I have to accept that there may not be an enforcement process that is even close to perfect. Although in principle platform-specific judicial decision-making is suspect, it may be that it is the only reasonably fair way to protect market competition in the face of phenomena like Amazon's and Google's platform domination.

There may, however, be a unique attribute of the Internet whereby government could encourage consumers to break monopolies when they act against the interests of consumers. That is, consumers usually have it in their power to switch from one provider of services to another. If they have information that a provider is acting against their interests, they have the means to retaliate.

That may be happening to Facebook contemporaneously. Government and commentators are bringing Facebook's policies regarding political advertising, for example, into the open. Users who think those policies are wrong can switch to another social platform or reduce their Facebook usage. If enough users switch, Facebook's dominance will cease.

That kind of consumer revolt—based on information—is uniquely capitalist. It is just like the corn flakes example, where consumers use their new information to determine the course of the market. I think that kind of consumer enforcement is better than law cases that grind on for years—maybe even decades.

Mergers and Acquisitions

The relative lack of relevance of the Sherman Act's antimonopoly provisions that the AT&T, IBM and Microsoft cases suggest, however, does not apply to Section 7 of the Clayton Act. That law should be enforced far more vigorously than it has been in the recent past.

After two Clayton Act Section 7 Supreme Court decisions in the 1960s— *Brown Shoe* and *Von's Grocery*—that enjoined acquisitions of companies with fairly minor market shares on the ground that the acquisitions tended toward "incipient" monopolies, free market economists fought back. They said that such injunctions not only interfered with the workings of the market but also prevented the accomplishment of beneficial economies of scale. The judicial backlash after the *Von's Grocery* case ended up making it impossible for the government to prevent business combinations except in extreme cases.

As many recent commentators have argued, that trend went way too far. The problem, as so often, is to fashion a principled way to distinguish between those business combinations that threaten to create monopolies and those that do not. This is a particularly acute question when large, dominant companies like Google/Alphabet acquire newer companies that have strong technologies but minor market shares. That is not an issue that the case law has prepared judges to deal with effectively. And a new theory needs to be applied because it is relatively inexpensive for a giant like Google to acquire (and thereby to silence) a potential competitor in its early stages, when its market share might be minimal.

"Between Google, Amazon, Apple, Facebook, and Microsoft, they have collectively bought over 436 companies and startups in the past 10 years, and regulators have not challenged any of them." Tepper at p. 106.

The Big Pharma companies also acquire small companies that may have world-beating drugs but no market share.

Companies that are dominant also use that dominance to erect defenses to competition. Some defenses are legal, such as patent protection. But some defenses are illegal—or arguably illegal, such as Google's tying practices that I mentioned a few pages ago. Those should be challenged. The closer the self-protecting company is to monopoly, the less leeway it should have to use questionable means to protect itself.

We also should recognize that managements have personal incentives to make acquisitions. Larger balance sheets usually mean larger compensation. Therefore, if you make a large acquisition, you tend to make more money, even though you may, as part of that acquisition process, borrow a great deal of money that makes your company more fragile in an economic downturn. Those thoughts are not strictly relevant to an antitrust discussion, but they are relevant in the larger public policy debate because they suggest that public policy should not assume that market efficiencies motivate acquisitions, as most free market advocates would contend. Other, less beneficial, motives frequently are paramount.

As I was writing this antitrust chapter,, yet another merger came across my radar screen: A proposed merger of McGraw-Hill Education and Cengage Learning—not quite household names that suggest monopoly. But they both are prominent in college textbooks and related media, and together they would be the number two firm in their field. The Wall Street Journal told it like it is:

"McGraw-Hill and Cengage expect their merger to yield $300 million of total cost savings over the next three years that they plan to use to expand digital offerings and lower prices. "We want to make the experience radically more affordable," Mr. Hansen [the designated head of the combined operation] said in the interview, foreshadowing what is likely to be an argument as to why regulators should sign off on a union of the rivals."

Do prices go down when industries become more concentrated? Theory says they will go up. Nor are there likely to be any significant economies of scale in publishing, where increased market power can increase profits without decreasing costs.

My purpose in this antitrust discussion is not to propose any particular way of dealing with the new problems. My purpose here is to suggest that antitrust is an important adjunct to market capitalism, that new technologies make application of the old laws quite difficult, and that, therefore, although not all new ideas are good ones, capitalism needs new ideas to protect the competition that forms the basic justification for permitting the market to govern so much of people's lives. Political will to protect consumers is a precious commodity.

Weeding out Fake News

Questions about the extent that companies like Facebook and Google that deal in information should be required—or permitted—to censor their content are not antitrust questions. They are questions the answers to which have to balance free speech against harmful consequences and private censorship against public censorship. It appears that most people think the online host companies should be the censors.

But I wonder that so many people seem to favor requiring private censorship of speech that the government might be prohibited from censoring.

Business Concentration and Worker Compensation

A substantial body of scholarly work has grown around the idea that increased business concentration has caused decreases in worker compensation. Tepper summarizes the assertions as follows:

> "Almost all the focus in industrial concentration has been on profits, productivity, and investment, but the biggest impact has been on wages. Workers have systematically lost power versus large companies that now dominate industries." (p. 37).

I think the point is not proven because there are so many other forces at work to reduce worker compensation, especially in fields where less than a great deal of education is required. My guess is that concentration is a minor factor compared with technological advance and foreign competition. As even Tepper noted (p. 46), the growth of technology companies that pay high salaries (but to much smaller workforces) has changed the aggregate worker income picture significantly.

I come back to the grocery business example that I discussed earlier: It is a very competitive business that includes foreign-owned stores such as Aldi and Lidl and, increasingly, Amazon, as well as other national competitors like Kroger and Walmart and regional competitors like H.E.B., Wegman's and Publix. The companies are large, sales volumes are large, but profit margins are thin. Despite the competition, wages are quite low, however, because of the thin margins and the nature of most of the jobs.

Even if business concentration has not been a major force in reducing worker incomes, however, it may be another factor that militates against permitting many business combinations.

I think we have to look elsewhere for ways to improve the incomes of less educated workers. There also are some simple things that could be done. One of them is to nationally outlaw non-compete agreements for employees earning less than some specified amount, as four states have done. (See Tepper at p. 68.) Non-compete agreements are, by their nature, anticompetitive.

CHAPTER 8

Beware The Great Nostalgia

Much of the current anti-capitalism movement is built on a nostalgia for the years after WWII when the U.S. economy was healthy, there was greater equality, greater national unity, and labor had more power. That nostalgia is misplaced. Every age has a supposed "golden age" to which it looks back with nostalgic envy. Today's golden age is the 1950s and the succeeding decade or two.

Here is James Pethokoukis of the AEI conservative think tank on that subject:

"Consider: America's postwar "golden age" economy—still pretty closed to trade and immigration—was built on prewar innovations and ephemeral, one-off dominance over war-ravaged industrial competitors. Of course those competitors were going to eventually recover. And that drawbridge-up economy meant complacent American industry then "collapsed at the first sniff of competition. So not a great model."

But many writers and politicians nevertheless refer to the 1950s and 1960s as a "golden age". Steven Pearlstein, for example, in his *Can American Capitalism Survive?* refers to the era as a golden age four times (pp. 49, 99,112 and 171), in each case advocating that America seek to return to the virtues of that time. ("Wouldn't it be fair and economically more efficient if the distribution of market income had remained more like it used to be," Pearlstein wishes at p.150.) Peter Georgescu, in his book *Capitalists, Arise!* also asks for a return to that era—or at least to its values.

Senator Marco Rubio, from the Republican side, says in a 40-page essay posted on his website:

"If private business is not investing to the extent it is expected to, the proper reaction should not be to overturn the American tradition for a new model, but to recover what has been lost. Doing so requires tracing our steps backward to better understand what that was, and how it was lost."

Unfortunately, Senator Rubio's essay never says how to do that.

In that golden age, great American companies took care of their workers and customers, not only their stockholders, it is widely alleged. Corporate leaders need to go back to that attitude—or else the government will force them to do so. That is the drumbeat that comes from many quarters.

As a veteran of the 1967 six-week strike by the UAW against Ford, I can tell you that with respect to the auto industry, that is hogwash. Labor and management both strove for a bigger piece of the pie. They were not looking out for each other. And as far as customers were concerned, the American automakers of the 1960s were fixated on competing with each other—customers were the measuring device, but it was not until Japanese competition came to America in the 1970s that the customer began to come first and innovation began. Was the auto industry unique? I doubt it.

Bloomberg columnist Justin Fox, in his book *The Myth of the Rational Market*, agrees:

"Big American companies reacted ponderously to the change in competitive environment brought on by the 1973-74 oil crisis and the less immediately obvious but even more significant rise of German and Japanese manufacturers. The stock market was of course much quicker to notice. Adjusted for inflation, the S&P 500 dropped even more from 1973 through 1977 than in the five years starting in 1929. The signals from the . . . market were clear. Corporate America needed to shape up. The question was how to get executives to pay attention." (pp. 162-63)

Pretty soon, the takeover artists and their ilk came along to wake up the complacent managers. By the mid-1970s they were in action, and by the mid-1980s, they were ascendant. See Justin Fox, *The Myth of the Rational Market* at p. 170.

The Golden Age—Not

Most civilizations in their declining years have had a concept of the Golden Age—or The Great Time. The Golden Age always was in the past, like 40 or 50 years ago or more.

Perhaps such nostalgia in recent times is a sign that America is in decline as a civilization. I hope not. The golden age, if it existed, is irretrievable. Let's not try to "make America great again". It never stopped being great.

In addition, there are many reasons we would not want to return to the 1950s, 1960s or 1970s, including less opportunity for black

Americans, less opportunity for women, lower living standards for everyone, etc. We should not let the imperfections of the present lead us to become nostalgic for a past that was not better. "Leave It To Beaver" may have a superficial attraction, but that world was relatively narrow, relatively repressed, and relatively poverty-stricken compared with today. That world led to the Women's Movement, the Civil Rights Movement, and the social upheaval of the 1960s—even eventually to Gay Pride and its success. The United States is a better place as a result.

Michael R. Strain of the AEI, writing for Bloomberg.com on the benefits of two-earner families, said:

> "Trumpian populism has intensified nostalgia for life in the 1950s, including family life. But who, even in the working class, would really trade places with someone living in 1953, with its much lower living standards and opportunities, and racial cruelties and injustices? Probably not many women, let alone racial minorities, that's for sure. And probably not many white men, for that matter."

Even after the Great Recession, most non-college graduates have said their standard of living is better than their parents'—and black and Hispanic Americans, despite all the discrimination that continues, say that is true by quite large majorities—68% and 70%, respectively.

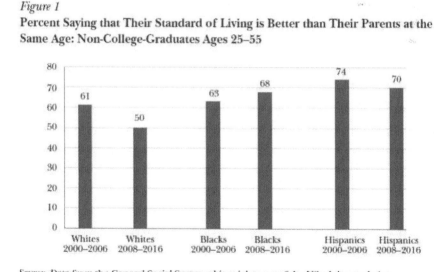

Figure 1

Percent Saying that Their Standard of Living is Better than Their Parents at the Same Age: Non-College-Graduates Ages 25–55

Source: Data from the General Social Survey, a biennial survey of the US adult population.
Note: Sample includes both men and women.

My source for this graph is "The Tenuous Attachments of Working-Class Men", by Kathryn Edin, Timothy Nelson, Andrew Cherlin, and Robert Francis, Journal of Economic Perspectives—Volume 33, Number 2—Spring 2019—Pages 211–228.

When we bash the capitalism of the 21st century, let us not do so in the hope of returning to the world of the 1950s. Vibrant civilizations look instead to a great future. America always has been a rambunctious, forward-looking nation. I believe that our nation and its civilization have a great future, but we can realize it only if we look forward to it and embrace the change that it will bring.

And maybe the "golden age" actually ended even before its advocates think it did—and before adoption of the policies of the Reagan Administration that often they blame for so much of labor's decline. According to the Bureau of Labor Statistics, real hourly earnings of production employees began to decline in 1973, as inflation took its toll on almost everyone's income. And the decline was substantially over by the time Reagan took office in 1981. And declines in manufacturing employment took place in other leading nations as well. Since 1990, American manufacturing employment has decreased 25%, but it has decreased 24% in Germany and 31% in Japan, as well.

The following graph created on the Federal Reserve Bank of St. Louis website doesn't go back as far as 1973, but it shows how the earnings of hourly and salaried men declined in the 1990s and again in the Great Recession, but comparable women's earnings continued to increase in the 1990s—presumably because they started from such a low level and gradually have improved as discrimination has lessened and women's education has overtaken men's. The top line represents men's earnings, the bottom line represents women's earnings, and the middle line is composite of the two.

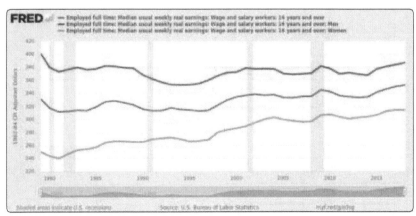

Hourly earnings of service employees remain lower than the hourly earnings of production employees. And the trend toward more service employment, as shown in the next graph (prepared on the Federal Reserve Bank of St. Louis website), has tended to make the overall trend in hourly earnings unfavorable.

The upper line is service employment. The lower line is manufacturing employment.

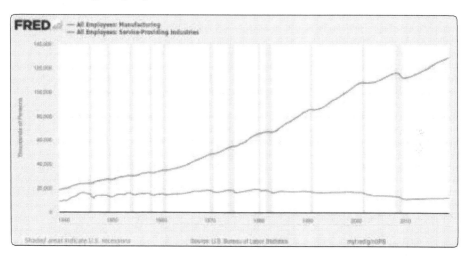

It appears to me that the trend toward service jobs (that pay less) may have been largely responsible for the nostalgia for the supposedly golden immediate post-WWII age. But that trend is not going to reverse because manufacturing will continue to become more efficient in terms of using people-power. Therefore America must assure that people get more and better education, so they can participate in higher paying work.

David Brooks has accurately summarized the forward-looking nature of the American project:

> "The real American idea is not xenophobic, nostalgic or racist; it is pluralistic, future-oriented and universal. America is exceptional precisely because it is the only nation on earth that defines itself by its future, not its past. America is exceptional because from the first its citizens saw themselves in a project that would have implications for all humankind. America is exceptional because it was launched with a dream to take the diverse many and make them one—e pluribus unum."

Since 1956, e pluribus unum is no longer our national motto, and it is no longer on my dollar bill, but we can still act as though it were.

*The world of the 1950s was
narrow, repressed, and poverty-stricken
compared with today.*

CHAPTER 9

Economic Justice

This line of discussion brings us to the currently hot topic of economic justice. What is it? Who decides what it is? Is it the same as Bernie Sanders' "fair deal" or my personal desire to be "fair" to those who don't flourish in life's competition? Is capitalism consistent with economic justice?

A British commission, sponsored by a left leaning think tank, published "Prosperity and justice: A plan for the new economy" in September 2018 (that I will refer to as the "British Report").

It provides a useful way to begin discussing those questions. Here are some of the British Report's findings, together with my brief reactions in brackets:

> ➢ Too many people are in insecure jobs. [Yes, secure jobs sound preferable, though I have never had one. I am reasonably sure that one would have to accept a reduced income to achieve additional security. But there is evidence that many people would give up a substantial percentage of their pay in exchange for greater security.]

> ➢ Receiving unemployment benefit is not the same as earning a wage: being unemployed deeply undermines most people's sense of self-worth and happiness. And an income from a job with little or no security–increasingly experienced in today's economy–confers much less wellbeing on most people than the same income from secure work. [Yes, employment is a good thing for most people. But, as I said, getting the same income from more secure work seems unlikely.]

> ➢ If we are to increase society's prosperity, we need to pay attention to the quality of work—and work–life balance, too. [Quality of life is indeed of paramount importance. I took a big pay cut a long time ago to achieve what I saw as a better quality of life. One should not expect the world to hand out a large income without sacrifice.]

➤ It used to be thought that prosperity and economic justice were in conflict; we had to choose one or other but could not have both. The international evidence now points in precisely the opposite direction. A more equal economy generates stronger and more stable growth, lower social costs and greater wellbeing. Both economics and morality argue for an economy that achieves prosperity and justice together. [I am not convinced by these assertions. The world's economies are quite various, and some nations that have fairly homogeneous populations have managed to create prosperity that was widely shared. I discussed some of this in the Corporate Governance chapter. I see no general relationship between the level of equality of incomes and the level of general prosperity, however, and the British Report's citations do not convince me.]

➤ It is not sufficient to seek to redress injustices and inequalities by redistribution through the tax and benefit system. They need to be tackled at their source, in the structures of the economy from which they arise. These include the labour market and wage bargaining, the ownership of capital and wealth, the governance of firms, the operation of the financial system and the rules that govern markets. Economic justice cannot be an afterthought; it must be built into the economy. [Yes, that would be a good plan. Unfortunately, the British Report does not include such a plan—only generalities—and, as they say, the Devil is in the details.]

➤ We do tend to think there is such a thing as society, that it can be in a better or worse condition, and that this affects how we feel ourselves. It is a striking fact that countries where these factors are perceived to be better are also those where individuals report themselves to be happier. [Agreed. How people perceive their society strongly influences how they feel about their own lives. A riven America is not conducive to Americans feeling good about themselves. This appears to be especially true of young Americans. The British Report contains no single definition of economic justice. It discusses many ways that economic justice would be different from the current state of the economy in the U.K. But missing is the road map of how to get to the described better places.]

The British Report states an admittedly Utopian "vision of the good economy". To me, that vision is so general and so Utopian that it is not very useful. But it is easy to see why people might yearn for it.

The British Report does have some concrete suggestions to carry out its program of economic justice. It proposes more diverse boards of directors, increased worker representation on boards, and simplified (lower) executive pay packages linked to "key drivers of long-term value" such as innovation and productivity, not just share prices. But in the end, I see no definition of economic justice that is better than saying merely that it would be more just than today's system. And, yes, today's system could be more just or fairer. But how to get there without impairing the good things about the current system is delicate. Many advocates of economic justice do not address the tradeoffs.

Regarding calls for new laws to require innovation, productivity and investment as opposed to short-term profit, I would point to how the market currently rewards those three long-term benefits—innovation, productivity and investment: The stock market's darlings over the last several years—the FAANGS—Facebook, Apple, Amazon, Netflix and Google/Alphabet—and Microsoft—all are among the biggest investors, the most innovative and the most productive companies in the world. Amazon, in particular, consistently sacrifices current earnings in the interests of long-term investments—and the stock market loves it, according Amazon not only a trillion dollar valuation but also the highest price-to-earnings multiple among the largest companies. Even Tesla, with negative earnings and negative cashflow, was a stock market darling because of its innovation and long-term investments (though personally I am skeptical of Tesla's long-term prospects).

A recent McKinsey study also tends to confirm that stock markets in various parts of the world reward long-term thinking.

Nevertheless, companies do not invest for the long term or innovate. Are their managements unaware that the market appreciates innovation, productivity and investment? If so, why are they unaware?

I do not think they are missing the message. It is more likely that those managements do not have the same level of imagination (and perhaps not the same quality of employees) and therefore do not think they can make successful innovative long-term investments. They may judge (possibly correctly) that they maximize long-term value by milking what they have. And if that is the case, society should let the market create newer companies that will have the innovative talent to supplant these milkers.

That in fact is what has been happening. The creative managers are investing for the long term. The managers without imagination are getting what they can out of tired franchises. Eventually, those tired companies fade away or are absorbed by others.

Many people are not happy about that reality, which is understandable. But capitalism remains the best attempt to make the most of reality and its limitations.

Economic Justice in America

Because it is so important, I will discuss again the equality of opportunity question that I discussed in Chapter 3:

Steven Pearlstein plausibly argues that there cannot be equality of opportunity. But his argument, after one redresses disparities of parental wealth, education and genetic legacy, boils down to an assertion that disparities of luck cannot be eliminated. Although it is true that disparities of luck cannot be eliminated, I hope I have argued persuasively that there nevertheless can be a meaningful goal of equality of opportunity.

Pearlstein's more fundamental point is that, "if we want an economic system that is fair and just, we have to go beyond the equalizing of opportunity to acknowledge the moral necessity of equalizing incomes in ways that make economic and moral sense." (p. 131) This is the argument that because equality of opportunity is not possible, society should create equality of outcomes. I addressed that in the earlier equality of opportunity discussion. I hope I convinced you that enforcing equality of outcomes was a bad idea. If not, please go back and look at the discussion in Chapter 3 again.

American economics Nobelist Joseph Stiglitz has used rhetoric that I find more appealing than Pearlstein's. In an April 19, 2019 New York Times op-ed, he called for a "progressive capitalism" that increases the safety net, increases government funds for education and job training, and increases funding for infrastructure.

In that article, Stiglitz is short on specifics, but one can see how to flesh out his suggestions in ways that will enhance both economic and personal growth. There can be a more just capitalism than we have now. It will not be Utopia. But it could be a capitalism that invests in its people, protects them when they might fall by the wayside, and invests in the infrastructure and environmental needs that can sustain prosperity and its best attributes. None of that is contrary to the capitalism that I have been defending and that I think Joe Stiglitz would defend in somewhat similar terms.

Guaranteed Annual Income and Similar Proposals

A perquisite that some Democrats (and some Republicans as well, perhaps) support is the guaranteed annual income or guaranteed job. Those concepts, regardless of what one calls them (I choose not to call them socialist, but many people might do so), may be antithetical to capitalism because they are not merely safety net provisions. The guaranteed income is a provision that would have the effect of making it unnecessary for people to work. Capitalism presumes that, as a general rule, people have an incentive to work in order to live. If one removes that incentive, one is removing a fairly fundamental assumption that underlies capitalism. (There also are many people, including me, who think that work is ennobling and part of leading a successful life.) I would rather provide a better safety net and better education, housing and health care than a guaranteed income.

Most Republicans (and many Democrats) reject the ideas of guaranteed income and guaranteed jobs.

The guaranteed job also has serious issues of practicality. Is the work done in the guaranteed job going to compete with work that is done by the private sector? Or is the government going to end up creating work that has little value? People might have been happy to dig ditches for the Civilian Conservation Corps in the 1930s. But would they be willing to do that in order to have a job today? What pride will people take in work that is the dole in another form? And what will the pay be? More than for an entry-level private sector job?

There have been and will be other ideas that, while they do not relate to placing the means of production within the control of the government, may be seen to damage fundamental underpinnings of how capitalism works to benefit people and the economy.

America does need to improve its safety net substantially. But in order to preserve the best aspects of capitalism and the overall prosperity that it bestows, the additional safety net provisions have to be tailored to reward work while softening the consequences for those who cannot find work. There are a number of such policies available, including increasing the amount that the government gives to people who work at low-paying jobs and providing a safety net of government makeup for workers who lose one job and take another at lower pay. Creating a better system of universal health care and strengthening housing assistance are two other ways to assure that people who are in low paying jobs or are out of work do not suffer more than necessary. Those are some of the many ways that a bigger safety net can be made without eliminating the incentives that capitalism may require for success.

I hope you will not mind that I do not enter the thicket of Supplemental Social Security for the disabled. The available facts simply are not sufficient to draw conclusions.

A 2019 article by leading sociologists Kathryn Edin (a professor at Princeton) and colleagues throws much needed light on the problems of less educated men. One of my takeaways is that less educated men in this decade do not really want to return to the type of work their fathers did, which was repetitive and, often, mind-numbing. They seek more creative and interesting ways to earning a living. Though many of them will not succeed in finding that more creative and interesting way, it is important for us to know what they are looking for—not a return to the world of their parents but a new world where they can gain greater self-realization. "The Tenuous Attachments of Working-Class Men", by Kathryn Edin, Timothy Nelson, Andrew Cherlin, and Robert Francis, Journal of Economic Perspectives—Volume 33, Number 2—Spring 2019—Pages 211–228.

Professor Edin *et al* conclude with sentiments that show that new thinking about economic justice is quite old—but vital nevertheless:

> "Of the transition from mechanical solidarity (agrarian societies, with bonds based on likeness) to organic solidarity (industrial and postindustrial societies, where bonds are based on difference) in the late 19th century, Durkheim [one of the founders of sociology] . . . wrote in 1897: "It has been rightly stated that morality ... is in the throes of an appalling crisis. [T]he remedy for the ill is nevertheless not to seek to revive traditions and practices that no longer correspond to present-day social conditions." Rather, he argued, "We need to introduce greater justice into their relationships by diminishing those external inequalities that are the source of our ills." To ease the crisis of working-class men in labor force attachment, ill health, and mortality more than a century later, we may need to do the same."

We do need creative thinking in order to rectify income and wealth imbalances without disrupting America's basic economic success. Such creative thinking should be and can be consistent with capitalism. And America could do that thinking and implement it successfully, if we had the mutual good will that it requires.

CHAPTER 10

Government Capture by Rich Cronies

One of the dangers posed by the enormous growth of the wealth of the top 1% or top .1% is their ability to capture important political positions or access to people in important positions. Money fuels election victories, so candidates and incumbents alike seek the favor of those who can contribute on a large scale. At the extreme, billionaires can form the core of a President's Cabinet. The dangers are many.

Crony capitalism is the name by which the principal dangers go. Markets guided by government in favor of the most affluent are the natural result. So, too, is tax policy that favors the wealthy, perhaps the most important aspect of which is estate tax policy that determines whether great fortunes are passed down through generations or split up, with charitable foundations receiving large parts of those fortunes. One of the knocks on French economist Thomas Piketty's analysis of wealth accumulation in *Capital in the Twenty-First Century* was that he ignored estate taxes. The 2017 U.S. Tax Act that eviscerated the Estate Tax has made it look like he may have been right to do so.

As I have pointed out several times now, crony capitalism is a perversion of capitalism that makes capitalism look similar to many other, inferior economic systems.

In a democracy, to prevent crony capitalism, it is simply up to the electorate to recognize what they are electing. That can be difficult in light of the complexity of today's issues and the amount of money that is invested in obfuscating them.

Caricatures of Capitalism

The capitalism that recent critics deride often is a caricature of capitalism.

The caricature of capitalism that seems to have prevailed since 2008 is of rapacious bankers misleading borrowers and investors to peddle financial products that enrich themselves but not the borrowers or investors. The caricature also portrays a system in which the rich get richer and the middle class gets stuck in low gear. It also is a system in which lavishly paid CEOs maximize their bottom lines at the expense of customers and workers. And worse, it is a system that fuels booms and busts that hurt ordinary people, but the perpetrators aren't punished.

These caricatures have sound bases in facts and data. The big banks *did* mislead investors and borrowers in the run-up to the Great Recession, the borrowers and investors *did* suffer adverse consequences, the rich *have* continued to get richer since the Great Recession, and the middle class has not participated appropriately in the economic progress made by the more affluent since 2009. In addition, the 2017 Tax Act that explicitly rewards owners of capital, the Trump Administration's rape of the Consumer Financial Protection Bureau (CFPB), and other recent acts by government tend to confirm that the moneyed classes have the power to benefit themselves at the expense of ordinary citizens. In doing so, they thumb their noses at the principles on which capitalism is based and declare that their actions are warranted by free markets and the necessity for investment incentives.

As I will discuss in more detail later, capitalism has a "money problem". People and institutions with money are able to do two things that the less affluent cannot do:

(1) They can invest and thereby grow their money.

(2) They can use their money to try to influence people in office and to get people elected who will share their view of the world and make policies and laws that will help them continue to grow their fortunes.

But these characteristics are not peculiar to capitalism. Whatever system people have adopted to govern their economies, the wealthy have sought to curry favor with the rulers, often paying them off (often covertly), in order to gain access to the best investment opportunities and in order to gain laws that are favorable to the moneyed classes. And, although there may have been minor exceptions, in all societies the wealthy have been at least somewhat successful in doing these things. Indeed, in non-democratic societies, they have been more successful than they have been in democratic capitalist nations.

Recent events have brought to the fore questions of when one thing is impliedly given in exchange for another. When is one thing a quid pro quo for something else? One can argue about the definition that applies in the criminal law. But the definition that applies in real life should not be as strict as the criminal law definition. In order to send someone to jail, we need to know beyond a reasonable doubt. We do not need to know that to judge people's actions for ourselves.

Anyone with experience in the world knows that a thing may be given with the expectation that another thing will be given in return without the bargain having to have been explicit. I urge you to believe that in terms of morality, an implied quid pro quo is the same as an explicit one.

Democratic capitalism has the means to prevent or ameliorate the ability of the wealthy to take control of the machinery of government and the means to prevent enormous wealth from becoming too ascendant. Those means are the ballot box and taxation. No matter how much the wealthy insist that taxation will be bad for the country, bad for growth, and therefore bad for ordinary people, ordinary people do not have to buy those assertions. Ordinary people do have the power to think and evaluate for themselves, to vote for candidates who will adopt policies that do not favor the wealthy, and thereby to enact laws that provide for suitable taxation of income and of intergenerational transfers of wealth. At some point, taxation *does* become onerous and counterproductive. But the rest of us should regard skeptically assertions about where that point is that are made by the wealthy or people in their employ.

Crony capitalism in which the financial elite has captured the mechanisms of government and, in the name of free markets, have twisted them for their own ends, is a natural danger. Indeed, it is natural enough that Adam Smith warned against it back in 1776. Today's crony capitalism is the greatest threat to capitalism since the fall of the Third Reich because its powerful advocates proclaim it to be ordained by the free markets that they claim are the basis of capitalism. Free markets are not the basis of capitalism. *Competitive* markets, regulated in the interests of consumers, are the basis of capitalism. And Americans should vote for that.

*Economists are not good
at predicting the future.
But who is good at it?
That's why it's called the future.*

CHAPTER 11

What Has Capitalism Accomplished and What Should We Expect It To Accomplish in the Future?

Basically, economic growth per person was stagnant throughout the world for many centuries until the 18th century. People's standard of living hardly improved from Roman times (say, 200 AD) to The Enlightenment (say, 1750)—a period of more than 1500 years! The standard of living then took off gradually in Britain, the U.S., the rest of Western Europe, and eventually in Japan, accelerating throughout the 19th century, and gathering even more momentum in the 20th century. Was this due to capitalism? Technology? Resources? Governance? Probably it was due to a combination that cannot be disentangled. But it is difficult to imagine such growth could have occurred without the ability of people to allocate resources through markets.

Here is an example of the virtuous paradigm: In the early 19th century, wages in Britain had increased and were higher than in most other places. That meant consumers could buy more things. And that ability made it worthwhile for the British to invent new things and processes. Those new things and processes increased productivity of workers, and the workers therefore earned more, leading to greater incentives to invent. And as invention increased productivity, workers made more again. Yes, some jobs disappeared or required fewer people, but the jobs that remained and the new jobs that were created paid more. This virtuous circle worked throughout the rest of the century from about 1830, and it created the largest boost in people's income and living standards in history. (See, for example, Stanford Professor Ian Morris's wonderful book, *Why The West Rules—For Now*. For a more technical economic approach, see Daron Acemoglu's article that I cited in Chapter 6: "Automation and New Tasks: How Technology Displaces and Reinstates Labor", Journal of Economic Perspectives—Volume 33, Number 2—Spring 2019—Pages 3–30.)

William J. Baumol, Robert E. Litan and Carl J. Schramm, in their 2007 (Yale University Press) book *Good Capitalism, Bad Capitalism, and the Economics of Growth and Prosperity*, explained succinctly how great the transformation has been:

"The most astonishing thing about the extraordinary outpouring of growth and innovation that the United States and other economies have achieved over the past two centuries is that it does not astonish us. Throughout most of human history, life expectancy was about half what it now is, or even less. We could not record voices or speech, so no one knows how Shakespeare sounded or how "to be or not to be" was pronounced. The streets of the greatest cities were dark every night. No one traveled on land faster than a horse could gallop. The battle of New Orleans took place after the peace treaty had been signed in Europe because General Andrew Jackson had no way of knowing this. In Europe, famines were expected about once a decade and the streets would be littered with corpses, and in American homes, every winter the ink in inkwells froze." (Kindle Locations 62-67).

* * *

"Economic growth has been . . . astounding. It is estimated that the purchasing power of an average American a century ago was one-tenth what it is today. A moment's thought will make you realize what a significant change has occurred in an individual's economic circumstances over the past few generations. Suppose you were accustomed to receiving the income of an average American today, and suddenly nine-tenths of it were confiscated." (Kindle Locations 71-74).

Places that did not adopt capitalism in the 19th century, such as Russia, China and India, did not achieve great economic success even if they had abundant natural resources. That does not prove you cannot have progress without capitalism, but it does beg the question, "If it was not the lack of a market economy, what prevented those great nations from flourishing?" Imperialism probably held India back, and the West's gunboat diplomacy probably held China back. But would they have adopted capitalism had those foreign interventions not taken place? I find it difficult to believe they would have done so, given their relative poverty, lack of universal education, and autocratic systems of governance.

India became a democracy in 1948, but its economy languished for about four decades after that, until it began to adopt a more market-oriented economy. Perhaps it was natural for the elite leaders of an India stratified by castes to believe that a more planned, more socialist economy would provide a better economy. But that did not work.

China only briefly had a republican form of government around 1912, but it remained backward through the ensuing authoritarian regimes of the Kuomintang and Communist Party, until the leadership of Deng Xiaoping in the 1980s. China since Deng seems to be a relative outlier in that, although it has a repressive regime and mixed economy that uses markets only intermittently, it has grown apace for about 40 years, taking it from poverty to middle income status and great national power. Is China the exception that proves that neither democracy nor a market economy is necessary for economic growth that benefits the people?

Perhaps. If so, what has enabled successive generations of Chinese autocrats to make decisions that have created economic benefit to the people of China, as well, of course, as creating some very wealthy people with good connections? Or is it the degree of market economy that has flourished alongside the state system that has made this possible? My guess is that China has demonstrated that in some circumstances, "socialism with Chinese characteristics"—that is, a mix of socialism and capitalism—can work. But in the Chinese case, it has not been accompanied by freedom of speech, the press or movement. How long will it continue to work?

According to data from Bloomberg.com, in 2018, 15,000 millionaires left China, mostly for Australia, Canada and the U.S. It appears that Chinese people with economic means fear that their wealth can be confiscated at any time.

What Should We Expect Capitalism to Accomplish in the Future?

Even if capitalism has been a major factor in accomplishing the enormous growth of the last two and a half centuries, is it necessary in order to accomplish continued growth of middle class incomes in the future? Or might there be a better system for allocating resources that would benefit a larger share of the population?

McKinsey Global Institute, a think tank backed by a large corporate consulting firm, predicts that the same process that worked for the last 250 years will work for the near future:

"Over the next ten to 15 years, the adoption of automation and AI technologies will transform the workplace as people increasingly interact with ever-smarter machines. These technologies, and that human-machine interaction, will bring numerous benefits in the form of higher productivity, GDP growth, improved corporate performance, and new prosperity, but they will also change the skills required of human workers."

I am not predicting McKinsey will be correct, but history is on their side. For a contrasting view by a great economist, see Tyler Cowen's chilling book, *Average Is Over*. In that book, Cowen predicted that 15% of the population will learn to co-opt machines and that the rest of the population will serve that 15%. I hope not. I hope that an American education explosion will make Cowen's bleak future inaccurate.

Wondering about the future, we should recognize that over the last 250 years, for the less affluent parts of the population, income growth has tended to be uneven and to depend not only on the economy but also on educational progress. There have been periods of relative stagnation and periods of significant progress, as education and the needs of the workplace go in and out of sync.

In the middle of the 21st century, economic progress for large segments of the population will again depend heavily on better education. And a better safety net will be needed for those whose education becomes redundant. The willingness of taxpayers to fund post-secondary education, as they funded secondary education beginning early in the 20th century, will be a key to the ability of American capitalism to provide economic progress to less affluent Americans in the mid-21st century, as it did in the 19th and 20th centuries.

China and India are funding education. Whether America will do so will depend on our resolve.

America has an urgent early education problem in that a large percentage of our less affluent children enter kindergarten substantially behind their more affluent peers. This disparity must be remedied if our less affluent children are to have a real chance to compete and to succeed in the 21st century world where education, more than ever, will determine whether a person has an opportunity to succeed at work. That is the main subject of my book *The Education Solution*. We can spend all we like on later education, but that will not succeed unless we overcome the early education deficit.

The relative stagnation of American middle class incomes over the period since 2000 frequently is cited as a modern failure of capitalism. That assertion is shortsighted. First, the introduction of competition from vast numbers of workers from elsewhere in the world has tended to dampen American wages. Those workers from elsewhere are now beginning to be able to buy more American goods and services and thereby they will add to American workers' incomes. Second, cultural changes have not been kind to the bottom third of Americans, who have fallen behind in the skills they need to compete technologically. The stagnation is important, but capitalism is not its major cause.

There are responsible economists who think that low economic growth is likely for the near future. For example, Neil Irwin of the New York Times has opined that, "The low-growth world was not just a phase. It's the new reality beneath every macroeconomic question and debate for the foreseeable future."

And Professor Robert J. Gordon of Northwestern has written extensively about what he sees as America's low growth future. See his masterful book *The Rise and Fall of American Growth*. It is an excellent history of our economic past. But I wonder about Professor Gordon's predictions.

My perspective suggests that the world has never known where the next innovation was going to come from. Therefore, the fact that we do not perceive the next major innovation today does not mean that, when it comes, it will not be as revolutionary as the steam engine or the digital computer.

A significant question is whether the incentives that capitalism provides are likely to be better than some other system for encouraging people to innovate. Looking at history, I would say that capitalism provides the best incentives—even recognizing that many innovations are made more out of pride than out of a desire for material wealth. I would venture to guess that even scientists who work at least as much for pride as for money do find that the prospect of money remains an incentive. In the U.S., even government workers who make significant contributions to innovations receive a part of the rewards—along with the government itself.

Industrial Policy

These thoughts bring me back to the anti-capitalistic subject of industrial policy. Early in this book, I suggested that an industrial policy such as Japan had in the 1970s and 1980s was eventually self-defeating. Now, some 40 years later, many American economists, politicians and pundits are admiring China's industrial policy and suggesting that America should emulate that policy in order to promote certain key industries. These pro-industrial policy advocates come both from the right and from the left. It is not a partisan issue at the moment.

I continue to be wary of government picking winners and supporting them. That almost inevitably leads to favoritism and political pork. But we should make a distinction between picking winners for government support, on the one hand, and supporting education and research in identifiable fields whose fruits will be available to all, on the other hand. The Internet did evolve from government-sponsored research. And the National Institutes of Health (NIH) is a great example of how public money for research can lead to benefits for people, not only in America but around the world.

The U.S. could very well create several institutes in the image of the NIH in various research fields. An institute dedicated to environmental research would make great sense. And institutes in many of the technological fields that the proposed industrial policies would support would make sense, too. These could include artificial intelligence and other aspects of computer science.

Basic science often is not ideally supported by private enterprise because the rewards appear only in the distant future, and thus an enterprise that properly is focused on profit making is not likely to undertake that research. And, as in medicine, once the basic research is done, American private enterprise in those fields will be willing and able to take over the practical development and marketing without further government assistance. There is plenty of private capital available for that kind of development.

The development of the vaccine against cervical cancer is an example of how this works. Researchers at NIH led development of the theory and spearheaded the initial proof of effectiveness. After that, large pharmaceutical companies were willing to pay for the expensive trials and development of mass manufacturing and to pay the NIH patent royalties for the privilege of marketing the vaccine.

Thus, following the example of our national institutes for health research would be very different from Japanese or Chinese industrial policy. But it could have important rewards both for consumers and for businesses.

CHAPTER 12

The Money Problem

For a modern discussion of money and its discontents, please see Morgan Ricks, *The Money Problem*. Or for a brief overview, see my review of that book at seekingalpha.com.

Finally, I am coming to the rapacious bankers that have caused so much of the reaction against what people perceive as "capitalism". I have divided the problems caused by finance into two sections. The first section deals with the concept of money itself. The second group of entries deals with the temptations that access to large amounts of money seems to pose for people.

Providing access to capital is among capitalism's best features. But in other respects, money, especially borrowed money, is a problem for capitalism, as it is for other economic systems as well.

The Peculiar Role of Money

Although money is the measure of the value of goods and services that makes the market capitalist system work, money itself is not created by a market mechanism in any nation. In all nations, it is created by the state— and within the state, in most nations, by an elite institution that is not elected by the people. In the U.S., that institution is called The Board of Governors of the Federal Reserve System—or usually just the Federal Reserve Board or the Fed.

Today, substantially all governments create what is called "fiat" money—that is money that is money only because the government says it is, and in most nations, no one but the government is permitted to issue money as narrowly defined. (Under some analyses, banks issue money, and under some broader analyses, anyone can issue money as more broadly defined by issuing an IOU in exchange for a credit on someone else's books.)

There is considerable nostalgia for monetary systems that were backed by gold (the last vestiges of which ended in 1971) because they have the appearance of greater stability. In fact, historically, they were not stable. For an excellent description of why and how it didn't work, see Amahad Liaquat, *Lords of Finance: The Bankers Who Broke the World* (Penguin Books 2009).

In effect, all monetary systems are unstable to a degree. The Bretton Woods system, for example, that was devised by the best economists in the world at the end of WWII, lasted only 27 years, from 1944 to 1971. The current basic system of market exchange rates between currencies has survived for almost 50 years, and, despite the indignities and privations that it visits on nations that do not keep their fiscal houses in order, it seems to be about as good as any system. In most cases, when a nation seeks greater stability for its currency by pegging it to another currency or basket of currencies, the market defeats the attempt. For example, the recent attempt by the Swiss to prevent the Swiss franc from appreciating by pegging it to the euro ended abruptly after just four years (2011-15), with the franc soaring in value—just what the Swiss had sought to avoid.

The instability of modern monetary exchange rates often plays a significant role in financial crises, however. Nations that borrow a lot of money denominated in a currency other than their own are subject to runs on their own currency if doubts about their ability to repay the foreign currency arise. And the abrupt devaluation of the local currency then tends to lead to economic privation. This happened to several Asian nations in 1997.

Is the U.S. monetary system, where an independent Federal Reserve Board manages the money supply, the ideal system? I do not know. No one seems to be able to define the money supply very usefully. Therefore, as I see it, the appointed group of wise people manages interest rates to grope toward a beneficial result—sometimes successfully. ("We were groping through a fog," wrote former Fed Chairman Alan Greenspan in his memoir (p. 156), describing a mid-1990s monetary policy decision.)

A recent blogpost by libertarian macro-economist John Cochrane of The Hoover Institution suggested that neither the Fed nor anyone else knows what the inflation rate is, despite the Fed making policy on the basis of it and many others arguing about whether the Fed has done the correct thing.

But the Fed does not trumpet its own shortcomings, Congress seems to expect the Fed to have an all-powerful grip on the economy, and most of the public therefore assumes that the Federal Reserve Board is, collectively, a financial wizard. So, popular reasoning goes, with all that power and ability, why the heck did they let the Great Recession and accompanying financial collapse occur? Something must be rotten in the Marriner Eccles Building (home of the Federal Reserve Board).

My answer is that the Fed governors (Fed board members are called governors) are humans trying to make sense of a complex system without a road map. Sometimes they lose their way.

Recently, an alternative theory—the Modern Monetary Theory (MMT)—has become attractive to some Democrats who seek to increase government spending to levels that they do not think taxation will support. MMT effectively says that printing money can be done in any amount, effectively forever, unless and until inflation takes hold—then it becomes necessary to increase taxes to stem the inflation. I doubt that the theory can be correct—and I wonder what happens to the economy when the eventual taxation regime comes in. For useful discussions of MMTs shortcomings, see, for example, a brief article by Colin Roche and a blogpost by John Cochrane. I find the Cochrane blogpost convincing. But another recent article by Martin Wolf of the FT also is convincing to the effect that MMT is correct but that the timing of when to begin taxing to stem inflation is politically dodgy.

However, Ray Dalio, head of the large hedge fund Bridgewater Associates, has outlined what he calls "MP3" (meaning the third modern iteration of monetary policy) that is similar in some respects to MMT and that, at least to me, seems to have clearer advantages over the current system.

At bottom, Dalio's MP3 would replace the Fed's tinkering with interest rates and buying securities in the open market with more targeted government spending that would be paid for by printing money rather than by increasing taxation or issuing debt. The great advantage of Dalio's MP3 is that it can target where the money goes—that is, the people who should get it or the governmental policies it should fund, such as education, infrastructure or the environment.

Dalio says:

"We also don't believe that monetary policy is producing adequate trickle-down. QE [quantitative easing] and interest rate cuts help the top earners more than the bottom (because they help drive up asset prices, helping those who already own a lot of assets). And those levers don't target the money to the things that would be good investments like education, infrastructure, and R&D."

That is all very attractive, provided it will not cause too much inflation. MP3's inflation control is complex. Maybe it would work—or not. I am not sure.

As Dalio points out, however, even if we like the possibilities of the MP3 system, it has to be implemented by a group of people who would have great discretion to spend and allocate people's money. Whom are we to trust? Which elite group? Congress? The Fed? Some new kind of body? I have no suggestion. But it is an issue that would need to be addressed.

Whatever our skepticism about MMT, both the U.S. government and the Chinese government seem to be testing an aspect of it (without saying so) and the Japanese legislature is debating its applicability to Japan. Both the U.S. and China are issuing debt in such large amounts that, unless MMT has at least some validity, the consequences will be quite adverse.

Regardless of one's skepticism about MMT, MP3 or the Fed's ability to manage the economy, however, it does not appear that a market-based solution is available. Thus we are left with the irony that the capitalist system that is based on humanism and democracy has to depend on an elite-driven board to manage the key instrument that enables the market to function. But that is not a defect that is peculiar to capitalism, since it seems that any economic system must have some person or entity that creates money and decides how much to create and how to allocate it.

There are people who claim that a crypto-currency usefully could change the way money works and would make it more market-oriented. I think it is too early to take that seriously.

Money Markets

A great deal of the money that the wealthy make comes through dealing in money—that is, by buying and selling money at wholesale.

The money markets are not governed by normal capitalist principles because consumers—the usual arbiters of allocations—are not present. They neither lend nor borrow at wholesale, and unlike wholesalers of goods, wholesalers of money mostly both buy and sell at wholesale, not eventually selling in smaller amounts.

In the years since 2000, the Fed has most of the time given forward guidance to the effect that short-term interest rates (the rates it can control) will remain low for extended periods of time. That gave the green light for those with access to money to borrow short and lend long, taking advantage of the yield curve in the safest securities. That was a boon that people with money gladly accepted, and it exaggerated inequality in America. Quantitative easing probably added even more to inequality.

Thus, money markets have a very different dynamic than markets in goods or services—and for that reason, require very different kinds of regulation.

One of the defects of macroeconomics is that historically it has not recognized this difference and the consequent importance of better regulation. That is beginning to change, as Morgan Ricks' excellent book has indicated. The government exercising better control of the money markets will not affect the benefits of capitalism because real investment is not buying money at one price and selling it at another, however complex that process may be.

There also is a respectable body of thought that says increased "financialization"—meaning more of a nation's income going to financial activities, as has been the case in the U.S. over the last 40 years—tends to impede increases in productivity. See, for example, Rana Faroohar's book, *Makers and Takers*. I am not persuaded that this is a significant problem. But it might be.

Dangers of Capitalist Finance—

There are many dangers posed by capitalist finance. I tend to think that the same or similar dangers exist in other systems of finance. (Money tends to corrupt.) But because capitalist finance is so much freer, its practitioners have used their ingenuity to create deleterious as well as advantageous products, services and practices. The next several sections will outline some of the dangers and their causes. Many of these issues cry out for better regulation.

After the Great Financial Crisis of 2008 (GFC), many people in Britain and America thought that major bankers would go to jail and that large banks would be broken up. Neither of those things happened. Nor did the heads of the largest banks (those that survived, anyway) have their remuneration cut substantially.

How could that be, people have wondered? How could it be that these people who had just perpetrated the worst financial crisis in four generations just get off scot-free and go on with business as usual?

The anger such questions generated has fueled populism on both the left and the right. And understandably so.

In order to better understand what happened and didn't happen—and what needs to be done within market capitalism to prevent recurrence of damaging booms and busts—the next few sections will analyze some of the various parts of banking that come under the general heading of "investment banking".

Those various businesses carry different risks and, just as important, seem to involve different levels of temptation to commit criminal acts in order to gain an economic advantage.

Unfortunately, I do not think the leading financiers themselves are going to be a part of the solution. Too many of them still believe they are entitled to the enormous amounts they get for their efforts. And the arrogance of many seems to know no bounds.

Borrowing Short to Lend Long or in a Currency that Is Not Your Own

A major vulnerability of the capitalist financial system—even though it has propelled the growth of economies—is its tendency to finance long-term financing needs with short-term borrowed money. That formula works when economic times are good, but it leads to the bankruptcy of key institutions when economic times become bad. The Great Recession of 2007-09 was a striking example of this tendency, when not only banks but also companies like General Electric's giant finance subsidiary GECC borrowed short and lent long as well.

The first thing one should say in response to attacks on capitalism based on the boom and bust of 2004-09 is that boom and bust cycles have been present in all societies for all of recorded history. They are not unique to capitalism. (The best history of boom and busts is *This Time Is Different* by Reinhart and Rogoff. It is a difficult read but rewarding.) Modern communications and the relative openness of capitalist societies have made the defects—and particularly the consequences—of borrowing short to lend long more obvious. But tricks of the securitization trade have made the fact that society was borrowing short to lend long less obvious, even to experts.

Previous attempts to make economic cycles less volatile have not succeeded. That is largely because (1) they have tried to make the system work without addressing the basic problem of borrowing short to lend long, and (2) they have focused primarily on shoring up the banking system rather than on the fundamental causes of boom and bust cycles.

Prominent economists, as recently as the 1990s, opined that the Fed could deal with busts; therefore they were not a big concern. That became the conventional wisdom. But it was wrong. When the crisis came in 2007, the Fed did not know what to do. The prediction that the Fed could deal with busts was so wrong that it should make us distrust economists' understanding of how money works.

Banks in all systems tend to borrow short to lend long and to under-reserve for bad loans. Thus the long-short problem and its accompanying boom-bust problem is almost universal. It exists even in the least liberal financial systems (such as China's).

The world has not yet fully recognized that financial booms are paid for with financial busts. Thus those who occupy positions of power—and who of course like remaining in power—work to create debt-fuelled booms, relying on the public's lack of understanding that the boom will be paid for—by them—when the bust ensues. President Erdogan of Turkey, for example, sowed the boom and now the Turkish people are reaping the bust.

Turkey and its corporations made the double mistake—a double mistake that has been made by many countries—of borrowing not only short but also in dollars rather than its own lira. It is basically the same double mistake that caused the "Asian Contagion" in Thailand, Malaysia, Indonesia and Korea in 1997 and devastated the economies of those nations.

Recent efforts to make financial systems safer have improved the strength of banks, especially in the U.S., but there remains insufficient recognition that "maturity transformation" and the practice of lending with borrowed money are the root causes of the instability. See my 2017 book, *Instability: The Fragility of Banks and What To Do About It*. Europe still must make its banks stronger, but so far it has not had the will to do so. Europe is not alone, however. Chinese and Russian banks also are overleveraged and under-reserved.

Are the Trump era federal government deficits leading toward the next economic bust? I do not know. But the risk is there.

Borrowing to Create and Economic Boom

The traditional part of banking (what we might call commercial and consumer banking) takes deposits and makes loans (or extends credit in other ways) and buys marketable securities for income. It also provides financial services to businesses and individuals. That is the part of banking that consistently commits the sin of borrowing short to lend long in order to increase the margin of what it is paid for credit it extends over what it pays for money. Commercial banking was not much involved in the frauds of 2003-06. (Unfortunately, more lately, Wells Fargo Bank has demonstrated that even its "plain vanilla" commercial and consumer bankers could commit organized frauds on their customers. And that has increased the world's—warranted—revulsion at the banker class.)

The borrowing that caused the economic boom of 2003-06 in the U.S. was mostly by individuals who borrowed to buy homes or to use the rising values of their homes as ATMs to obtain money to spend on other things. The government also was borrowing copious amounts of money to fund the wars in Iraq and Afghanistan, as well as the War on Terror at home. In *Debt Spiral*, I have a table (at p, 7) that shows that without the excess borrowing (that is, borrowing that was greater than normal) there would have been no boom. The economy would have had almost no growth in 2003-2006.

The edifice of prosperity (only four years, really, since the last recession) crumbled when house prices began to fall in late 2005. The home loans that had been made in 2003-05 (and continuing into 2006) had not been made to withstand *any* decline in house prices.

Whereas in previous eras, lenders had been cautious about lending only an amount that the borrower could repay based on his/her current incomes, and only in an amount that was significantly lower than the current value of the house, lending in the brief boom period ignored those normal principles. Loans were made to people who could not repay, their incomes were not verified, loans were made with interest rates that would rise precipitously after the first year or two, and loans were made at or near 100% of the appraised value of the house.

How could lenders have been so stupid as to change the way they had done business for the last 50 years? I tell that story at length in *Debt Spiral*—you do not need it all here. The important point about what happened is that the market, not lenders, was making most of the loans in the brief boom period. And the market included not only American institutions that bought the securities into which the mortgage loans had been packaged, but also many European banks and other institutions that were buying.

Because in most lending institutions, securities are bought by a different group of people from the people that make loans, the officers in charge of buying the securities did not view their activities as making loans or as requiring the same type of analysis as making loans. They saw themselves as buyers of securities that happened to be backed by loans. (Does that sound weird? Yes it does. But that's the way it was. Banks—especially big banks—tend to have different silos that make loans and buy securities. If they talk to each other, probably it is mostly about last week's football game.)

Thus, the ultimate funders of the loans were not doing any work to look out for themselves. They were just buying securities based on their high ratings and relatively high coupons in relation to their ratings (as if there were a free lunch—higher coupon without higher risk—no, no free lunch). And if they were not looking out for themselves, who was? The answer turns out to be "no one", including the rating agencies. And that was why the process turned so ugly.

The typical chain through which a loan was made included a mortgage broker who had the contacts with the borrower, the mortgage bank that bought the loan, the investment banker who, together with an aggregator, packaged the loan and created securities based on it, the credit bureau that rated the various securities into which the loan had been made, the underwriter who sold the securities in the global capital markets (usually the same investment banker who created the securities structure), and, ultimately, the securities buyer—where the money came from. (Actually, the securities buyer may also have been borrowing that money from somewhere else, too.)

There were a lot of people feeding at the trough. But up and down the line, they were neither the borrower's nor the ultimate buyer's friend. Mortgage brokers, almost throughout the country, were committing fraud at the very outset of the process. They were encouraging homeowners to lie about their assets and their incomes. They were helping homeowners prepare false papers to do that. The mortgage bankers would buy anything, so long as it met the stated criteria of the investment bankers and aggregators—and the mortgage broker fraud made sure the standards were met. The investment bankers would sell anything that the credit bureaus would rate AA or AAA. And the credit bureaus, the "gate keepers" that the ultimate buyers depended on, loved the deal flow that the investment bankers were giving them. So they cut corners, made bad assumptions, and failed to do their fundamental job: to protect the market.

As the process continued through 2003-05, house prices rose, construction boomed, and speculation became rife. Prices simply should not go up that fast. And more houses were built than in any other period in American history.

Many of the investment bankers/underwriters committed what I would call fraud against the ultimate buyers because they knew the securities should not have had the high ratings that they had been given and did not disclose that to the buyers. Indeed, it seems they did whatever they could to conceal it. The major underwriting banks settled the law suits brought against them, but both the large amounts for which they settled and the one opinion regarding a minor underwriter that went to trial suggest that where there was smoke there was fire. The underwriters were culpable.

Of course, the ultimate buyers of the securities were not the only ones who suffered. As house prices declined and owners were unable to pay their mortgages, a foreclosure tsunami ensued, and the Great Recession caused a cascade of woe. And it all started because of the debt-fueled boom.

But that terrible process should not lead us to be nostalgic for the cozy, inefficient financial system we had in 1970. New regulatory processes are needed to control the new possibilities, but those new policies should not be the kind of 1950s-1960s financial repression that blew up in the 1970s.

Too Big To Fail

One of the great resentments that stemmed from the GFC was at the government assistance that enabled some of the biggest banks not to fail. Commentators of many kinds have railed against policies that treat some banks as too big to fail (TBTF). I have written about this phenomenon extensively, including in *Debt Spiral* and in *Instability*.

TBTF is not a new concept. It originated in the early 1980s, when the government did not permit Continental Illinois Bank to fail. It was the eleventh largest bank in the U.S. and could have been dealt with by more usual means if allowed to fail. Probably the way it was dealt with was bad policy.

Less explicitly, at the same time, the Fed went light in its treatment of Citibank and some other large banks that had made loans to South American countries in the naïve belief that "sovereigns do not default". They do and they did. And the naïve large American banks were left with a large amount of bad loans. If they had reserved fully for those loans, they might have been insolvent. The Fed, however, went slow in its regulatory process and nursed them back to life with the help of the U.S. Treasury. Good or bad policy? I could argue either side. But regardless of which side would be correct, I would wonder why it is fair for Citi to have gotten kid gloves treatment when smaller banks did not get that kind of treatment at the same time.

What happened in 2008 was more extreme. Not only America but the whole Western world was suffering from a crisis of confidence in the financial system. Additional failures of large financial institutions probably would have caused commerce to slow dramatically, with the consequences that many more people would have been laid off, many more companies would have gone bankrupt, and the cycle of defaults and foreclosures in the housing system would have been made even worse than it was.

In those circumstances, the lesser evil was to prevent additional large banks—both in the U.S. and Europe—from failing. That was not ideal because it created what economists call moral hazard and it led many people (quite sensibly) to resent that the banks were "bailed out" when so many consumers were allowed to lose their homes to foreclosures. But it was the right thing to do so in the circumstances. And if it makes anyone feel better, most of the CEOs of the banks that might have failed lost their jobs. Moreover, the government got all its money back, with interest, so maybe we should think of the capital injections as good investments.

Is TBTF a permanent fixture of capitalism? I think so. But I also think that it is a permanent fixture of any economic system. There are circumstances in which large financial institutions are critical to the functioning of the economy—regardless of who owns the financial institutions—be it government or the private sector. And, no, breaking up the largest banks, however satisfying that may sound, would not solve the problem. In a major financial crisis, there comes a point when the next failure, even one of relatively modest size, might tip the economy into relative free fall. My preference is to try to understand what causes financial crises and to use that knowledge to try to avoid them. I have written about that in *Instability*.

Investment Banking

A set of financial activities that is different from commercial and consumer banking goes under the heading of "investment banking". But that category itself has several very distinct businesses. They include underwriting securities, trading in securities, and financial advisory business, primarily regarding mergers and acquisitions.

The underwriting business was where the biggest frauds of 2004-07 took place. The underwriters created securities that were hard to understand, convinced the rating agencies to give those securities high ratings, and then sold the securities to institutions that were misled as to the securities' creditworthiness. That process was central to creating the 2003-06 boom and therefore was central to creating the bust that we call the Great Recession.

Committing securities fraud is capitalism run amok. But both European statism and American lax regulation laid the foundations on which the frauds were built.

The complex securities were so much in demand because the European banks were awash in cash in the years immediately after the advent of the euro. A euro was supposed to be a euro of the same value regardless of in what eurozone nation it was deposited. That meant that in practice the nations would have to rescue their banks if they got into trouble, and the money markets relied on that by providing wholesale financing to European banks on an unprecedented scale. No longer were European banks reliant on deposits; they could borrow in the wholesale markets and grow their balance sheets at will. Nor did capital requirements restrain their growth very much because Basel II capital requirements (that had just come into force in Europe but were not in force in the U.S.) were lax and flexible. Thus the European banks became the main purchasers of the CDO securities that the investment bankers created with the badly underwritten mortgage loans. Yes, although not widely known, that is what happened: the European banks financed the U.S. housing boom, as well, incidentally, as the similar booms (and busts) in Spain and Ireland.

Some of the details shed light on the relationship between capitalism and state sponsorship of financial intermediaries. The next few paragraphs are pretty wonky, so skip them if you are not interested in these details.

European statism and lax American (and derivatively, German) regulation led to creation of Special Investment Vehicles (SIVs) by a number of banks, but most prominently by German Landesbanks that were among the first to fail and be state-rescued in August 2007.

The Landesbank story can help us to see that it was not only capitalism that failed but also statism and the governmental promotion of lending. The Landesbanks had been established by the German states to support lending to the Mittelstand, small and medium-sized German manufacturers. The sates guaranteed the Landesbanks' liabilities so they could borrow at low rates and therefore lend at low rates. But two things happened:

(1) As capital markets developed, the Mittelstand companies became able to borrow from other sources, so the Landesbanks had no real reason for being.

(2) The EU decided that the outright state guarantees were not permitted, so they were repealed, leading to increases in Landesbanks' borrowing costs.

But although the Landesbanks were left with no natural way to make money, the moral obligations of the states to support them remained.

Thus, when in 2004-06, investment banks explained to several Landesbanks how they could make a profit on an arbitrage between long-term CDOs (the securities into which the mortgages had been stuffed) and short-term ABCP (asset-backed commercial paper) using the effective guarantee of the sponsoring Landesbank, it was an easy sell. The problem was that in 2007 when the market saw the weakness of the CDOs—and therefore refused to roll over the ABCP—the effective guarantees were called, the Landesbanks failed, and the German states were left having to step up and carry out their moral obligations to bail out the Landesbanks and thereby to protect the Landesbanks' creditors. One does not have to understand all these details in order to see my point: Subsidized lenders get taken advantage of, and the subsidizing state ends up the biggest loser. In this case, both of the bugaboos of borrowing short to lend long and borrowing in a currency that is not one's own were at work.

Why did the German central bank permit the Landesbanks to incur those guarantees? Because the Fed and other U.S. banking authorities had done so for U.S. banks "in order to promote lending and thereby to help the economy". The guarantees that the U.S. and German regulators expressly permitted significantly magnified the size of the boom—and therefore of the bust.

Subsidies—including subsidies for lending—effectively violate the basic principles of capitalism. Subsidies substitute the dictates of an elite for the workings of the market. And often, subsidized lenders lead to expensive failures, as at the Landesbanks in 2007, Fannie Mae and Freddie Mac in 2008, the S&Ls in the 1980s, and in Europe at banks like the Franco-Belgian government-owned Dexia (a provider of municipal finance) in 2011.

Mergers and Acquisitions

Another aspect of investment banking is advising on mergers and acquisitions. Over the last half century there have been a number of specialized companies that devoted themselves exclusively to this type of advisory practice. They have demonstrated that if their personnel can get the trust of corporate managements, they can provide advice at high prices with relatively low risk to themselves. Thus, the M&A business is, in and of itself, not dangerous to the financial health of a large banking entity that owns it.

The corporate world at large, however, has a much more fraught relationship with its M&A bankers.

As I discussed in the chapter on antitrust above, many mergers and acquisitions make economic sense to the parties to the transaction because they dampen competition. But those deals often are bad for the economy as a whole.

There is another entire class of M&A deals that end up being bad for the acquiring company over the long term. But the incentive system makes it too attractive for companies to be acquirers—and the M&A bankers are experts at playing on those incentives.

The biggest such incentive is the benefit to a CEO and his C-Suite staff (yes, usually it is his) of being big. Quite simply, by being big, a CEO and his staff are likely to make more money.

But usually it is not in shareholders' interests to make acquisitions with stock. The dilution to existing shareholders usually makes the deal look too expensive. Therefore, most deals are done for cash. And usually that is more cash than the acquirer has in its bank accounts, so it has to borrow—usually substantial amounts. That suits the M&A bankers just fine because they will get a fee for helping to arrange the debt financing.

But the debt also will make the corporation more fragile in the event of an economic downturn. That is, the acquiring corporation will have to pay the interest (and any amortization) on the loan regardless of its cashflow's adequacy. Therefore when cashflow gets crimped, the corporation's business and investments in the future get crimped. Frequently, that means that although the stock may go up immediately after the merger, it goes down in subsequent years.

M&A bankers know all about this. It is their job to make the deals happen anyway.

Trading

Another investment banking business is trading. It was in trading where the participants from several major banks colluded to jigger the price of money, as represented by LIBOR, EURIBOR, etc. Trading is, in my opinion, prone to illegal activity because so much money can be made from such small pricing differences and because the community of traders is so small, even though it is global.

Trading exists in all societies and all financial systems. But the modern investment bank and the modern hedge fund have brought it to a level of profitability that has attracted among the brightest people in the world. Some commentators say traders' activities are socially useless. That conclusion would be debated by economists who find that the liquidity and price discovery they provide to markets is socially useful. But I agree that the amounts of money traders can make are stunningly greater than any social benefit that I can see. And securities and derivatives trading are not necessary parts of capitalism, even if they do help to establish prices and create liquidity.

We should recognize, however, the enormity of the amount of capital that modern investment banks employ. The change from even the 1980s is mind-boggling. To take a simple example, I recall an acquaintance doing a $200 million dollar deal in the late 1980s to take a company private. It was a big deal! It was a signal accomplishment. Today a deal ten times that size would be piffle. 100 times that size would be an average deal. Similarly, traders who 30 years ago might command a trading account in the millions now command trading accounts in the billions. Compensation reflects the amounts of money that can be made or lost.

Whose money is it that these traders can make or lose? It is not theirs. It is the shareholders' money. Most investment banks are public companies whose stock is widely held by institutions such as pension funds, endowments, insurance companies and mutual funds. Hedge funds get most of their equity money from the same kinds of institutions. Thus it is the public's money—though disproportionately the more affluent public's money. The outsized pay comes from their (our) pockets, but we pay it willingly if the investment banks we own (or the funds they run) succeed.

But here is where the competition comes in: The competition for the jobs managing those vast sums is ferocious. Many of the brightest people in the world compete for those jobs. Thus, whether they have any social utility or not, the system is highly competitive. And the pay is for performance.

I said above that the capitalist system of finance is a necessary part of capitalism because the alternative—state allocation of capital—leads to the financial system financing the things that elites want instead of things that the market (people) wants. China is challenging the statement I just made in that it is using a largely state-based financing system to create what the elites think is good for the people—though not without a great deal of graft that tends to corrupt what gets built. The vision of high-speed rail, sparkling airports, pristine roads, and vast new buildings complexes can be defended as being in the long-term best interests of the Chinese people because all those infrastructure projects should create economic activity and rising employment and wages in the future. That the U.S. does not do such things on as broad a scale is not, however, due to capitalist finance.

U.S. capitalism embraces the idea that much infrastructure should be built with government money. But the infrastructure does not get built because Congress is unwilling to impose the necessary taxes. If that unwillingness to impose necessary taxes is due to American moneyed elites having captured the machinery of government, then we have merely crony capitalism with American characteristics. If Americans want better infrastructure, they will have to learn to vote more in their long-term best interests. Unlike the Chinese people, we do have choices to make.

Beware When Government Encourages Lending

Despite government's central role in creating money, when government plays a role in allocating the use of money for lending, the effort often leads to a bad outcome. I described earlier what happened when the banking regulators bent the rules to encourage more lending in the 2000s: The loans were not made according to normal standards and they defaulted in unprecedented numbers. On a similarly large scale, the government engaged in financial repression in the 30 years after WWII, largely in order to encourage money to flow into housing loans. That repression led to the S&Ls (whose charters dedicated them to housing finance) borrowing short to lend long (that was government policy), and when interest rates rose precipitously at the end of the 1970s, the situation threatened the solvency of almost all of America's home lenders.

In the late 1970s, government encouraged America's largest banks to "recycle" "petrodollars" by lending to South American nations that needed the money for development. The idea sounded good. Take the money deposited by the oil-rich nations of the Middle East and invest it where it was needed. The only problem was that in fairly short order, the South American nations began to default, and that threatened the solvency of some of America's largest banks.

There are more examples of how government encouraging lending has backfired. But a few examples are enough to see the picture.

Money is peculiar stuff. It is not like anything else. Everybody wants it. Therefore almost everybody is willing to borrow it. But repaying it is another matter. A creditor has to be disciplined in making loans in order to make money at it. When government makes it seem too easy or offers rewards other than just getting paid back with interest, discipline erodes and, often, insolvency beckons.

CHAPTER 13

How the Business Corporation and Capital Markets Helped to Create America

It is usual to credit the building of America to vast land and natural resources and the resourcefulness of the American people (who came from all over). Credit also should go, however, to a *third pillar of American success*: the invention of the general business corporation law and, with that, the development of the most extensive capital markets in the world. It is those business developments that enabled American enterprises to build railroads across the country, create companies that manufactured myriad products, and enabled people to invest in those kinds of enterprises.

Until New York passed the first general corporation law in the early 1800s, there was no simple way for people starting a business to invest without opening themselves to unlimited liability for the debts of the business. Either they had to form a partnership with unlimited liability or apply to a legislature or sovereign for a charter for a limited liability company. That system was deeply undemocratic because only the wellborn or very well connected could get such a charter. That situation both prevented competition and entrenched the wealthy.

The general corporation law, which fairly quickly spread to other states from New York, permitted anyone to obtain a corporate charter for a fairly modest fee—and through that corporate charter, to conduct business without having to effectively guarantee the debts that the business might incur. This new avenue was open to immigrants from anywhere as well as to more established Americans. Thus it was a great leveler.

But the general corporation law also enabled the business to sell stock to investors and thereby to raise substantial capital without the investors being subject to liability for more than they had invested. And that propelled the stock market and business.

Today America has the most extensive and deepest capital markets in the world—and it is those markets that permit American companies to raise the capital to create global enterprises as well as local ones. (Local enterprises are harder to find capital for because they are dependent on a small geographic area and a few key employees. Thus, almost everywhere in the world, policy makers wring their hands over the relative dearth of capital for small and medium-sized businesses. The fault usually lies not in the financial system but in the relative riskiness of smaller enterprises.)

One should contrast the American capital markets with the relative weakness of capital markets in the rest of the world, where businesses seeking capital more often have to turn to banks for funding. That matters a great deal because banks are not (or should not be) risk takers. They should lend only to sound credits. (Banks also tend to be run by elites that are more likely to lend to their own kind.) Without deep capital markets, good projects are far more likely to go unfunded.

The first pillar of American success is the abundant land bounded by two oceans. The second pillar of American success is the immigrants who mostly came from across those oceans. The third pillar of American success is capitalism.

CHAPTER 14

Ethics and Capitalism

The clear ethical violations committed by investment bankers and traders in the years just before the GFC and that have been committed by Wells Fargo bankers more recently have raised in many minds the question whether capitalism itself is not so infected with self-interest that its participants cannot be ethical.

Capitalism cannot deny self-interest, since its theory is based on a belief in individual self-interest and, in the aggregate, its power to create a better material world. But self-interest as a consumer versus self-interest as a citizen in other parts of one's life sets up a difficult dichotomy.

Capitalism is debased when secrecy and poor ethics overcome transparency and consumer choice.

The frauds of 2004-06 and the fixing of LIBOR, EURIBOR etc. show the temptations that derive from money being one's business.

I have observed such temptations for more than 50 years in law and business, and I have been disappointed in the ethics of many people in business—not only in financial businesses. Indeed, I often have been disappointed in the ethics of people in general (and sometimes, in hindsight, even in my own).

But although capitalism has to learn to do better, please look around the world at other economic systems! Everywhere it is true that power corrupts and that absolute power corrupts absolutely. That is the fault of human nature, not the fault of capitalism.

According to Confucius,

"Truth may not depart from human nature. If what is regarded as truth departs from human nature, it may not be regarded as truth."

(Quoted by Robert J. Barbera in *The Cost of Capitalism*)

Ethical standards the world over are low. Petty bribery takes place in business every day in every country, and it grows in scale the more government is involved in business. Thus, although I cannot defend the ethics of capitalists, I do aver that the ethics of other types of economic systems tend to be worse.

Some of the bribery is out in the open. It is just that the government and business worlds do not think it is bribery.

I will aver further that the rot begins at the top. If senior people in government or business are seen as lining their own pockets at the expense of those they serve, pretty soon the excuse is heard throughout the land, "Everybody else does it." And that persists until some reforming prosecutor wins some high-profile cases.

Trust and Social Capital

Many modern philosophers advocate that "social capital" is essential to a happy and productive society. There are many definitions of social capital, but they have in common a shared set of understandings within a society. In the view of many commentators, the trust that shared understandings generates that is paramount.

General acceptance of an economic system (such as capitalism) is an essential part of a society's social capital. If a large part of society does not accept the mechanisms through which assets and liabilities are allocated, then trust in general is damaged.

There are other aspects of social capital and cohesion than economic systems. And in many ways, other aspects are paramount in people's minds.

This essay has dealt only with the economic system under which the United States is governed, not those many other aspects of national cohesion or division. But I hope that in the limited area of economics, this book's discussions have convinced at least some citizens who have doubted capitalism's usefulness that it can work in interests of all of us. And, similarly, I hope that those discussions have convinced some citizens who have embraced the free market mantra to see that both effective regulation to protect consumers and a fair safety net are necessary to enable capitalism to flourish.

Building trust is essential in order for what has become a fairly fractured society to become happier and more cohesive. Differences of opinion there always have been and always will be; that is not the issue. The issue is whether we can believe that our disagreements are legitimate, not borne of malevolence or sloth.

In addition, even in the 21st century, some needs of the community have to be commonly understood in order for a democratic society to be able to defend itself. A set of shared common values remains the best guarantor of freedom. See Professor Muller's *The Mind and the Market* at p.13 for some historical background to this idea.

The Moral Basis of Capitalism

Ayn Rand (a 20th century best-selling novelist who hosted an old-fashioned intellectual "salon" in New York) and her acolytes saw a moral basis in capitalism through the rubric of freedom—"free markets" was their mantra. The problem with such a formulation is that it is simplistic. It justifies all the worst aspects of capitalism as well as the best, as I have tried to show.

Some economists have seen a moral basis in capitalism because people earn an amount that is their "just deserts". I discussed that earlier and rejected it on the ground that luck plays such a big part in what anyone has at the outset of life, as well as what happens thereafter.

But Rand was correct that an economic system should have an ethical or moral as well as an economic or pragmatic basis.

The moral basis for capitalism is that wherever competition can be present, it relies on the decisions of ordinary people, not elites, to allocate resources and set prices. In the absence of a competitive market, capitalism cedes ground to the elites in government to provide next-best solutions.

Market capitalism is fundamentally an affirmation of humanism and pluralism. It also recognizes that capitalism's excesses have to be curbed by laws that make markets less free but more competitive and more transparent.

All human institutions are imperfect. The questions social scientists wrestle with are how to create institutions that work for large majorities of people to help them to live productive lives with respect and freedom from unwarranted intrusion. In creating such institutions, contradictions are inevitable. It is only through persistent good will that we can succeed in charting the most useful course through this rapidly changing world.

Selected Bibliography

Acemoglu, Daron and James Robinson, *Why Nations Fail* (Currency 2012)

Acemoglu, Daron and Pascual Restrepo "Automation and New Tasks: How Technology Displaces and Reinstates Labor", Journal of Economic Perspectives—Volume 33, Number 2—Spring 2019—Pages 3–30

Autor, David H. "Work of the Past, Work of the Future", AEA Papers and Proceedings 2019, 109: 1–32

Barbera, Robert J., The Cost of Capitalism: Understanding Market Mayhem and Stabilizing our Economic Future (McGraw-Hill Education 2009)

Baumol, William J, Robert E. Litan and Carl J. Schramm, Good Capitalism, Bad Capitalism, and the Economics of Growth and Prosperity, (Yale University Press 2007)

Brownell, Charles, Subprime Meltdown: From U.S. Liquidity Crisis to Global Recession (2008)

Brock, H. Woody, American Gridlock: Why The Right and Left Are Both Wrong; Commonsense 101 Solutions to the Economic Crises (Wiley 2012)

Chancellor, Edward, Devil Take the Hindmost: A History of Financial Speculation (Plume 2000)

Cooper, George, The Origin of Financial Crises (Vintage Books 2008)

Cowen, Tyler, Average Is Over: Powering America Beyond the Age of the Great Stagnation (Plume 2013)

Donkin, Richard, Blood, Sweat & Tears: The Evolution of Work (Texere 2001)

Duncan, Richard, The New Depression: The Breakdown of the Paper Money Economy (Wiley 2012)

Ebenstein, Lanny, Chicagonomics: The Evolution of Chicago Free Market Economics (St. Martin's Press 2015)

Edin, Kathryn, Timothy Nelson, Andrew Cherlin, and Robert Francis "The Tenuous Attachments of Working-Class Men", by, Journal of Economic Perspectives—Volume 33, Number 2—Spring 2019—Pages 211–228.

El-Erian, Mohamed, When Markets Collide ((McGraw-Hill 2008)

Faroohar, Rana, Makers and Takers; The Rise of Finance and the Fall of American Business (Crown 2016)

Ferguson, Niall, The Ascent of Money: A Financial History of the World (Penguin Press 2008)

Fox, Justin, *The Myth of the Rational Market* (Harper Business 2009)

Georgescu, Peter and David Dorsey, Capitalists, Arise! End Economic Inequality, Grow the Middle Class, Heal the Nation (Berrett-Koehler Publishers 2017)

Gordon, Robert J., The Rise and Fall of American Growth: The U.S. Standard of Living since the Civil War (Princeton University Press 2017)

Gorton, Gary B. Misunderstanding Financial Crises: Why We Don't See Them Coming ((Oxford University Press 2012)

Greenspan, Alan The Age of Turbulence: Adventures in a New World (Penguin Books 2008)

Greenspan, Alan, and Adrian Woolridge, Capitalism in America: A History (Penguin Press 2018)

Kindleberger, Charles P. ,and Robert Z. Aliber, Manias, Panics, and Crashes: A History of Financial Crises, Sixth Edition (Palgrave Macmillan 2011)

Liaquat, Ahamed, Lords of Finance: The Bankers Who Broke the World (Penguin Books 2009)

Lowenstein, Roger, The End of Wall Street (Penguin Press 2010)

Lowenstein, Roger, When Genius Failed: The Rise and Fall of Long-Term Capital Management (Random House 2000)

Lowy, Martin, Debt Spiral: How Credit Failed Capitalism (Public Policy Press 2009)

Lowy, Martin, Instability: Why Banks Are Fragile and What to Do About It (Public Policy Press 2017)

Lowy, Martin, High Rollers: Inside the Savings and Loan Debacle (Praeger 1991)

Lowy, Martin, The Education Solution: Restoring Prosperity; Reducing Inequality (Public Policy Press 2015)

Magnus, George, Red Flags: Why Xi's China Is In Jeopardy (Yale University Press 2018)

Meltzer, Alan H., Why Capitalism? (Oxford University Press 2012)

Minsky, Hyman, Stabilizing an Unstable Economy (McGraw-Hill Education 1986 and 2008)

Morris, Charles R., The Trillion Dollar Meltdown: Easy Money, High Rollers, and the Great Credit Crash (Public Affairs 2008)

Morris, Ian, Why The West Rules—For Now (Farrar, Straus & Giroux 2010)

Muller, Jerry Z., The Mind And The Market (Anchor 2007)

Noah, Timothy, The Great Divergence: America's Growing Inequality Crisis and What We Can Do About It (2012)

Paulson, Henry M., Jr., On The Brink: Inside the Race to Stop the Collapse of the Global Financial System (Business Plus 2010)

Patterson, James T., Restless Giant: The United States from Watergate to Bush v. Gore (Oxford University Press 2005)

Pearlstein, Steven, Can American Capitalism Survive? Why Greed Is Not Good, Opportunity is Not Equal, and Fairness Won't Make Us Poor (St. Martin's Press 2018)

Piketty, Thomas, Capital in the Twenty-First Century (Harvard University Press 2013)

Pollock, Alex J., Finance and Philosophy: Why We're Always Surprised (Paul Dry Books 2018)

Posner, Richard A., A Failure of Capitalism: The Crisis of '08 and the Descent Into Depression (Harvard University Press 2009)

Pozen, Robert C., "Curbing Short-Termism in Corporate America: Focus on Executive Compensation", Governance Studies at Brookings, May 2014

Prasad, Eswar S., The DollarTrap (Princeton University Press 2014)

Putnam, Robert D., Our Kids: The American Dream in Crisis (Simon & Schuster 2015)

Reinhart, Carmen M., and Kenneth S. Rogoff, This Time Is Different: Eight Centuries of Financial Folly (Princeton University Press 2009)

Ricks, Morgan, The Money Problem: Rethinking Financial Regulation (University of Chicago Press 2016)

Rifkin, Jeremy, The End of Work: Technology, Jobs and Your Future (Tarcher Putnam 1996)

Sassoon, Donald, The Anxious Triumph: A Global History of Capitalism 1860-2014 (Allen Lane 2019)

Ritholtz, Barry, Bailout Nation: How Greed and Easy Money Corrupted Wall Street and Shook the World economy (Wiley 2009)

Sawhill, Isabel, The Forgotten Americans: An Economic Agenda for a Divided Nation (Yale 2018)

Shiller, Robert J., The New Financial Order: Risk in the 21st Century (Princeton University Press 2003)

Smith, Adam, The Wealth of Nations (1776) republished in many editions

Smithers, Andrew, The Road to Recovery: How and Why Economic Policy Must Change (Wiley 2013)

Sorkin, Andrew Ross, Too Big To Fail (Penguin, 2009, 2010)

Sperling, Gene, The Pro-Growth Progressive: An Economic Strategy for Shared Prosperity (Simon & Schuster 2005)

Stiglitz, Joseph E., Free Fall: America, Free Markets, and the Sinking of the World Economy (Norton 2010)

Tepper, Jonathan, and Denise Hearn, The Myth of Capitalism: Monopolies and the Death of Competition (Wiley 2018)

Tooze, Adam, Crashed: How a Decade of Financial Crises Changed the World (Viking 2018)

Wilson, Kevin "Saving Capitalism: Some Modest Proposals", seekingalpha.com, May 24, 2019

Wolf, Martin, "The case for capitalism", Financial Times, March 28, 2019, a review of two books on the subject

Wolf, Martin, Fixing Global Finance (Johns Hopkins University Press 2008)

Woods, Thomas E., Jr., Meltdown: A Free-Market Look at Why the Stock Market Collapsed, the Economy Tanked, and the Government Bailouts Will Make things Worse (Regnery 2009)

Young, Stephen, Moral Capitalism: Reconciling Private interest with the Public Good (Berrett-Koehler Publishers 2003)

Zingales, Louis, A Capitalism for the People: Recapturing the Lost Genius of American Prosperity (Basic Books 2012)

Made in the USA
Lexington, KY
05 December 2019